THE INDEPEN
GUIDE T(
DISNEYLAND
PARIS 2025

G. COSTA

Limit of Liability and Disclaimer of Warranty:
The publisher and the author have used their best efforts in preparing this book, and the information provided herein is provided "as is." Independent Guides and the author make no representation or warranties with respect to the accuracy or completeness of the contents of this book and specifically disclaims any implied warranties of merchantability or fitness for any particular purpose and shall in no event be liable for any loss of profit or any other commercial damage, including but not limited to special, incidental, consequential, or other damages. Please read all signs before entering attractions, as well as the terms and conditions of any companies used. Prices are approximate, and do fluctuate.

Copyright Notice:
Contents copyright (C) 2012-2025 Independent Guides. All rights reserved. No part of this document or the related files may be reproduced or transmitted in any form, by any means (electronic, photocopying, recording, or otherwise) without the prior written permission of the publisher, unless it is for personal use. Some images and text copyright (C) The Walt Disney Company and its affiliates and subsidiaries. This guide is not a The Walt Disney Company product, nor is it endorsed by the said company.

Contents

Introduction

Disneyland Paris is Europe's most popular destination, having amassed over 375 million visitors since it opened in 1992.

The project for the resort started in the 1980s when Disney executives wanted to bring the magic of Disney theme parks to Europe. This was where the original stories originated, which inspired many Disney fairy tales.

Disney soon decided to build the resort in France due to its central location and favourable weather compared to some countries further north in Europe.

The fact that the site was less than a two-hour flight from many European locations sealed the deal. Plus, the French government promised to build infrastructure to make it easy to access the resort.

Disneyland Park opened in 1992 as a European adaptation of California's Disneyland. However,

Disney updated the design to reflect the local culture and took advantage of all the land the company had purchased.

The project had its critics. In 2002, the resort expanded with *Walt Disney Studios Park* becoming the second park at the resort, providing a portal for movie fanatics.

As well as the two theme parks, guests can enjoy the *Disney Village* area (free admission), with shopping and dining experiences that cover a range of tastes.

A campsite with an adventure playground and six themed hotels are also on site.

Disneyland Paris is not just a theme park or a place to ride rollercoasters. Guests can meet characters, watch shows and parades, make new friends and enjoy a feeling of magic that no other theme park resort in Europe rivals.

Thrill-seekers may not find the tallest and fastest rides in Europe here, but the quality of the experiences offered is second to none.

Disneyland Paris is a place where dreams really do come true for guests every single day, and you are about to become part of it all.

Planning

Planning a trip to Disneyland Paris may seem daunting. You must consider transport, accommodation, food, park tickets, spending money, and more. This section aims to get you prepared before we delve into more detail.

When to Visit

Disneyland Paris's crowds vary significantly from season to season and even day to day. The difference in a single day can save you hundreds of euros, as well as hours in queues. You'll need to consider national and school holidays across Europe, the weather, pricing and more to find the best time to go. Here is our guide to the best times to visit Disneyland Paris, even including which days of the week are the best.

MAJOR HOLIDAYS (TIMES TO AVOID)

In 2025
• 1st to 5th January: New Year's Day & School Break
• 15th February to 2nd March: French and UK school break
• 17th March: St. Patrick's Day (seasonal events mean slightly bigger crowds)
• 5th to 21st April: Easter Holidays
• 1st and 8th to 12th May: National Holidays and Ascension Day weekend
• 18th to 20th May: Pentecost/Whit Sunday
• 7th June to 7th September: European School Summer Break. August is the busiest month. July is much busier than June. September is less busy from the 1st onwards.
• 14th July: Bastille Day (Bank Holiday)
• 15th August: Assumption Day
• September and October

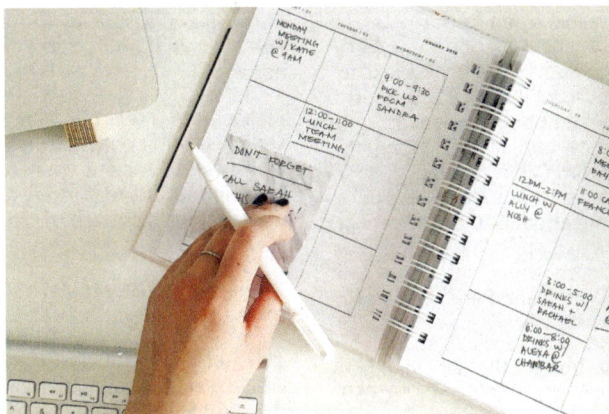

weekends
• 18th October to 2nd November: UK and France school holidays, and Halloween
• 9th to 11th November - Armistice Day Weekend
• 20th December 2024 to 4th January 2025 - Christmas Holidays. 31st Dec is the busiest day in this period.

Top Tip: If a public holiday falls on a Friday or a Monday, that weekend becomes a *pont* (a long weekend). If it is on a Thursday or Tuesday, many people turn this into a 4-day weekend. Avoid *ponts* as they are always very busy.

Days of the Week

The days of the week you choose to visit significantly affect how long you wait to get on rides. A ride can have a wait time of 90 minutes on one day and just 30 minutes on the next. The most notable difference is between weekends and weekdays.

The best day of the week to visit is typically Tuesday, followed by Thursday, then Wednesday, then Monday, Friday, and Sunday - the busiest day of the week is, by far, Saturday. Park hours are often extended on weekends to compensate for the larger crowds.

Doing Disney on a Budget

A visit to Disneyland Paris is expensive – it is a premium theme park destination. With travel, park tickets, accommodation, food and souvenirs, it is easy to see why many families save up for a long time for their trip.

However, there are many ways to reduce your spending at the resort yet still have a magical time.

1. Drive – Visitors from Europe can drive to the resort. Even from the UK, driving is an option - a ferry or Eurotunnel crossing can cost as little as £180 return when booked in advance for a car and all its passengers. From Calais, in France, it is an easy 3-hour drive. There are about €10 of tolls each way, depending on the route from Calais to Disneyland Paris, plus petrol costs.

2. Budget flights – Flights are available from £40/€50 each way from across Europe to Paris. *Charles de Gaulle* is the most convenient airport, followed by *Orly* airport. Steer clear of *Paris Beauvais-Tille* Airport, which is 120km from Disneyland Paris.

3. Take the train – TGV and Eurostar trains can get you to the resort. If travelling across France, try *InOui* (at sncf-connect.com), which offers affordable travel on high-speed trains from stations across France.

TGV advance fares are also often good value. You will arrive at *Marne la Vallée – Chessy* station.

Guests in the south of the UK have the option of Eurostar trains starting at £170 return if booked in advance.

Please note direct Eurostar services from London to Disneyland Paris ended in summer 2023 and journeys now require a change of trains.

Trains avoid costly transfers to and from airports.

4. Hotels – The official Disney hotels keep you in the bubble with their theming. However, they are expensive compared to nearby hotels, such as *Campanile Val de France* and *B&B Hotel at Disneyland Paris*. On the flip side, a non-Disney hotel means no *Extra Magic Time* (see page 33) and buying park tickets separately if you do not book a package via Disneyland Paris.

Alternatively, stay at a cheaper Disney hotel, such as the *Hotel Cheyenne* or *Hotel Santa Fe*, to get the on-site benefits.

5. Buy an annual pass – If visiting for at least four days, an annual pass can

work out cheaper than a 4-day ticket, especially when you take into account dining and merchandise discounts.

6. Use a special offer – There are often special offers running, whether it is 'kids go free', or an extra day and night free.

7. Tickets – Certain visit dates are cheaper than others, so if you have flexibility, visit during the off-peak season when admissions tickets are more affordable.

8. Eat at Disney Village – *McDonald's, Earl of Sandwich, Vapiano* and *Five Guys* sell fast food at prices cheaper than the food in the theme parks.

9. Meal Plans – If you eat at restaurants daily, pre-purchasing Meal Plans can save you money. They can be added at the time of booking or any time before your trip if you are staying at a Disney hotel. Plans must be purchased for the entire stay.

10. Packed lunches – Make your own packed lunches. A hypermarket called *Auchan* is in the nearby town of *Val* d'Europe. This is a 30-minute walk from the theme parks or a 5-minute bus, train or taxi journey. Alternatively, bring food and snacks from home.

11. Take your own photos – Skip the official character photo and take one yourself; the Cast Members (Disney employees) will even take the photo for you. If you want official photos, see our section on Disneyland Paris' PhotoPass and PhotoPass+ services for unlimited images for a set price instead of paying €15-€20 for each one.

12. Take your own merchandise – Buy dresses, outfits and toys from Disney Stores, online or at supermarkets before you visit Disneyland Paris. Give your child the costume or toy once you arrive to avoid the inflated in-park merchandise prices.

13. More affordable meals – Although food prices are high, some restaurants offer better value than others. Try the set menus with a main course, dessert and drink for one price. Or, try a buffet as a late lunch and have a lighter dinner.

Speaking French

All Cast Members at the resort speak French. With very few exceptions, the vast majority of Cast Members at the resort also speak English.

Therefore, for the most part, there is no language barrier when talking to staff.

However, knowing some basic French phrases is helpful. Employees appreciate it if you say Bonjour and then switch to English, or even better say Parlez-vous Anglais? [pronounced par-lay-voo-zarn-glay] for "Do you speak English?".

You may occasionally come across a Cast Member with limited English, which can make things more difficult but not impossible.

Cast Members hail from all across Europe and often speak other languages – Spanish and Italian, for example, are very common.

Useful French Phrases

Hello/Good morning – Bonjour [Bon-sjur]
Good evening – Bonsoir [Bon-swahrr]
Goodbye - Au revoir [Or re-vwarr]
Do you speak English? – Parlez-vous anglais? [Parr-lay voo-zarn-glay]
How much does this cost? – Combien ça coûte? [Comb-yeah Sar Coot]
Please – S'il vous plaît [Sill voo-play]
Thanks – Merci! [Mare-see]
No problem – De rien [De ree-yurr]
A photo, please? – Une photo, s'il vous plaît? [Oon photo sill voo-play]
Yes – Oui [We]
No – Non [Noh]
A little / a bit – Un peu [Erm purr]
One - Un [uh]
Two - Deux [dur]
Three - Trois [Trr-wah]
Four - Quatre [Cat-re]
Five - Cinq [Sunk]
Rare (for meat) – Saignante [Say-narnte]
Medium-Rare (for meat) – À pointe [Ah pwarnt]
Well-done/well-cooked (for meat) – Bien Cuite [Bee-yen kweet]
Very well-cooked (for meat) – Très Bien Cuite [Treh bee-yen kweet]

One very useful phrase you will need to understand when boarding rides is:
Vous êtes combien? [voo zettes com-byer] - This means, "How many are in your group?"

Currency and Payment Methods

France uses Euros as its currency. If you come from a country that does not use Euros as its currency, you can exchange cash before you go or use a debit/credit card while in France.

With payment cards, be aware of any fees from your bank for paying in a foreign currency. These are commonly around 2.9% per transaction.

Be sure to warn your bank you will be travelling to avoid your card being blocked for security reasons. One option for visitors from the UK is to use *CurrenSea* - a debit card that reduces fees to just 0.5% or less when abroad. Spend on the card as you would back home, and you will be charged to your UK bank account in pounds. The card is free.

Sign up with coupon code "GDSNES", and you'll get £10 free when you spend £100 abroad within four months of signing up. That's free money you can spend on some treats!

Alternatively, you may want to find a credit or debit card with 0% foreign exchange fees.

For guests who prefer to exchange money, all Disney Hotels also offer 24-hour currency exchange points at their reception desks, though expect rates to be less than perfect.

Celebrating Birthdays

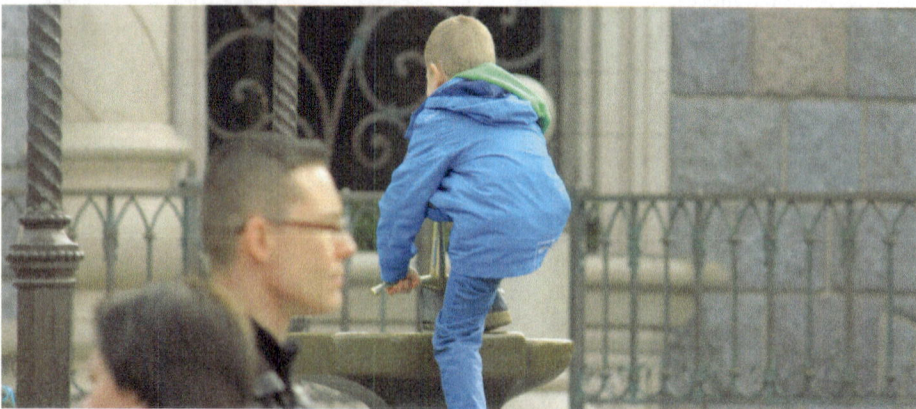

There are several ways to celebrate a birthday at Disneyland Paris. For example, at Table Service and Buffet restaurants, you can add a birthday cake to your meal for €45 (serves 6). A smaller dessert for 2 people is €25.

We recommend making a restaurant reservation by calling the dining booking line and mentioning the cake in advance - you can do this up to 2 months before the big day.

You can also visit Guest Relations (*City Hall* and *Studio Services*) to get a 'Happy Birthday' badge to wear during your special day.

To entertain younger guests, ask the *Cast Members* at *City Hall* whether any of the characters have a special birthday message for your child.

You will enter a room where a phone will ring. When your child picks the phone up, there will be a recorded message wishing them a happy birthday – what a fun idea!

Getting There

Travelling to Disneyland Paris is simple due to its central location. Options include driving, flying and high-speed trains.

Plane

Flying to Paris is convenient for many visitors as the French capital is under two hours away from most of Europe. Paris has three airports you fly into:

Charles-de-Gaulle Airport
This is the main Parisian airport and the largest.

o *By High-Speed TGV Train*: From the airport, catch a direct *Ouigo* or *InOui* train from CDG Terminal 2 to *Marne-La-Vallee – Chessy (Disneyland)* station in just 8-12 minutes. Pre-book at sncf-connect.com/en-en/. Tickets are €16-19 per person on *OuiGo*. Tickets are the same price with *InOui* if booked *fewer* than 10 days before travel - further in advance tickets are €37. The first train is around 06:50; there are no direct TGV trains after 20:30 (check the schedule online by making a test booking). We recommend buying tickets at the airport in case of flight delays.

o *By Local RER Train*: From the airport, take the RER B line to *Châtelet-les-Halles* station, then switch to the RER A line to *Marne La Vallée – Chessy*. €13 per adult with a travel time of 1 hour 30 minutes. Children under 10 years of age pay €6,50, and children under 4 travel free.
o *By Coach:* The Magical Shuttle bus goes between

the airport, Disneyland Paris and many *Val d'Europe*-area hotels. There are 17 daily journeys in each direction. €24 per adult each way and €11 per child. The journey takes about 1 hour. Book at magicalshuttle.co.uk. This is not a Disney-run service.
o By Taxi: €75 to €95 each way. This is a well-priced and convenient option for groups.

Orly Airport
Paris' second-largest airport.

o *By Coach*: The Magical Shuttle bus is €24 per adult each way, children pay €11. Coach transfers take about 1 hour each way. Book at magicalshuttle.co.uk. This is not a Disney-run service.
o *By Local RER Train*: Take the Metro Line 14 train to *Gare de Lyon* station. From here, take the RER A line to *Marne la Vallée – Chessy (Disneyland)* station. The total journey time is 1 hour and 20 minutes. This journey costs €13 per adult and €6,50 per child.
o *By Taxi/Private Van*: €75 to €105 for parties of 3 to 8 people. This is the cheapest and most comfortable choice for groups.

Paris Beauvais-Tille Airport
This airport is *not* in Paris and has long transfer times. It is where some budget airlines are based.

o *By Public Transport*: Get the *Terravision* shuttle bus from Beauvais Airport to *Porte Maillot* bus station. This is €16.90 each way per adult or child, infants (0 to 3) go free. This bus journey takes 1 hour 30 minutes. At *Porte Maillot*, follow the signs to the Metro and take Line 1 (yellow) to *Charles de Gaule - Etoile* (3 minutes).

At *La Defense,* take the RER A line (red) to *Marne La Vallée – Chessy (Disneyland)* station (40 to 50 minutes – costs €2.50 per adult, €1.25 per child). The total journey time is about 2 hours and the total cost is about €19.50 per person.

o *By Shuttle Service*: RSTransports.com offers a shared or private shuttle from the airport. Prices start at €101 for 4 people. Journey time is around 1 hour 15 minutes.

o *By Taxi*: The taxi fare is about €180 to €200 each way. Alternatively, you can rent a car. The journey is 126km each way.

Train

The Eurostar is the most comfortable option for visitors from the south of the UK, reaching the doorstep of Disneyland Paris in just 3 hours from London.

Please note that direct Eurostar train services to Disneyland Paris were discontinued in summer 2023 and it is not known when (or if) these will return.

Eurostar connecting via Lille:
Passengers board a Eurostar train in the UK (usually with the destination of Brussels) and disembark at *Lille Europe* station - about 1 hour and 20 minutes from London. At *Lille Europe,* passengers wait around 30 minutes for their connecting TGV train from *Lille Europe* to *Marne la Vallée - Chessy* Station (Disneyland).

The whole journey takes as little as 2h58m from London with a 34-minute stopover. Some stopovers are longer, so your journey may take up to 4 hours 6 minutes.

The Eurostar website usually shows connecting trains up to 12 weeks in advance.

Changing trains is easy - you look for the number of your next train on the departure board and go to that platform. Thirty minutes is plenty of time to change, as there are no security or immigration checks here and there are only 4 platforms. When on the platform, check that you are on the correct train, as there may be multiple trains on the same platform.

If one of your trains is delayed, you will be put on the next one at no extra charge.

The TGV train from *Lille - Europe* makes several stops. It only stops at *Marne-La-Vallee - Chessy* (Disneyland) for a few minutes - it is not the end of the route so be ready to get off in advance.

There is a helpful video of this process available from 'Disneyland Paris Advice' on Youtube called "Eurostar indirect via Lille".

International Train + RER (via central Paris):
Disneyland Paris is about 32km from central Paris, and the city centre is connected to the theme parks by the fast and frequent RER train service.

This means you can get a high-speed international train to Paris city centre, followed by a local RER train

Top Tip

Do not book your Eurostar travel with Disneyland Paris as part of a package without checking prices direct with Eurostar. It is often significantly more expensive to book transportation with Disneyland Paris. We recommend booking your train directly at www.eurostar.com. The exception is when Disney has an offer such as free travel for children when it can be cheaper to book with Disneyland Paris. As such, we recommend you check both options. You can book Eurostar trains between 3 and 6 months in advance, depending on the season and route.

to Disneyland Paris.

This offers you a lot of flexibility – for example, there are up to 18 Eurostar departures per day from London to Paris.

If arriving at *Paris – Gare du Nord* station by Eurostar, it takes a further 50 to 60 minutes to reach Disneyland Paris.

A ticket on the Paris RER train from *Gare du Nord* to *Marne-La-Vallée* (Disneyland Paris) costs €2.50 per adult and €1.25 for a child under 10 years old. Follow the signs at *Gare du Nord* for 'Metro & RER' trains.

Driving

You have two options to reach Disneyland Paris when driving from the UK.

The Eurotunnel is a train service that allows passengers and vehicles to travel together from Folkestone (England) and arrive in Calais (France) in 35 minutes.

Alternatively, you can take your car on the ferry from Dover (England) to Calais (France). P&O Ferries is a popular company. The ferry crossing is often cheaper than the Eurotunnel but takes about 90 minutes.

From Calais, it is a 3 hour 30-minute drive to Disneyland Paris. This 290km (180 mi) journey will cost about €10 in tolls and €30 to €50 in fuel each way.

Take the RER B line toward *Robinson*, *Antony* or S*aint Rémy-lès-Chevreuse* and get off after one stop, *Châtelet-Les Halles*. Here you transfer to RER A line by walking over to the adjacent platform and getting a train in the direction of *Marne La Vallée – Chessy*.

Use the information screens to check that the train is going to *Marne La Vallée – Chessy* station (your destination) as the line splits.

Marne La Vallée - Chessy (Disneyland) is the last stop on the RER A line. This journey takes about 40 minutes.

Disneyland Paris has a huge car park for both theme parks. The price of parking for a day is €30 for cars, €25 for motorcycles and €40 for motorhomes. Premium parking spots are €45 per day.

You will have free parking at your hotel and the entrance to the Disney theme parks if you are staying at one of the Disney hotels or the *Explorers Hotel*.

For those staying in other partner hotels, the cost is €30 per day (however, if you book your stay through Disneyland Paris, parking is free). The parking lot typically opens at 8:00 a.m. and closes 30 minutes after the closure of both parks.

Disney Express
If you have booked your train as part of a package with Disney, you will have the *Disney Express* luggage transfer service included. This allows you to drop off your bags at the train station on arrival and head straight to the parks.

At *Marne-La-Vallée* Station, follow the signs to the *Disney Express* counters on the top floor (open 8:00 am to 9:30 pm daily).

Here, you check in for your hotel and receive your *MagicPass* (digital park tickets, room key and Meal Plans). Leave your bags with the *Cast Members* at the desk and they will be taken to the luggage storage area in your hotel. Now, enjoy the theme parks!

This service is for all hotel Guests, whether arriving at Marne-La-Vallée/Chessy station by train or RER local train, by Magical Shuttle airport transfer or any other vehicle.

If you booked your transportation separately, this service is available for €18 per person each way.

The service is available from 7:45am to 9:00pm when sending luggage to the hotel. When leaving, luggage must be dropped at the hotel by 11:00am and can be picked up between 1:00pm and 9:00pm at the station.

Hotels

Disneyland Paris owns and operates seven on-site resort hotels, each themed to a different part of America – one is even a campsite where you can stay in log cabins. When booking a hotel directly with Disneyland Paris, your hotel price includes your park entry tickets.

Advantages of staying at a Disneyland Paris hotel:
• A front desk staffed 24 hours a day
• Friendly *Cast Members* with knowledge of the resort
• The option to pre-pay for all your meals at the hotel and the theme parks.
• Detailed theming and total immersion
• A stay in the heart of the Disney magic
• *Extra Magic Time* is available daily. *EMT* allows hotel guests entry into one or both parks one hour before other guests. During *EMT*, attraction wait times are very short or non-existent. See page 33 for more details.
• Walking distance to the theme parks: 20 minutes or less.
• Free shuttle service from all the hotels to the theme parks (except *Disney's Davy Crockett Ranch*)
• Meet Disney characters at the hotel during your stay.
• *Disney Shopping Service*: If you buy merchandise in the parks, you can have it delivered to your hotel to be collected in the evening, leaving your hands free.
• Park admission tickets are included in all reservations unless otherwise stated.
• Complimentary Wi-Fi in all guest rooms

Dining Key:
€ (Under €16)
€€ (€16 to €29)
€€€ (€30 to €39)
€€€€ (€40 to €49)
€€€€€ (€50+)

Prices relate to set menus for one person where available.

PRMP = Some options on the menu are available on the Premium Meal Plan
PLMP = Some options on the menu are available on the Plus Meal Plan
STMP = Some options on the menu are available on the Standard Meal Plan

Learn more about Meal Plans on page 39.

Hotel Package Pricing:
When booking your hotel, your arrival date determines the price for your entire stay (e.g. if you arrive on a date within the Value pricing season and the remaining days of your holiday are in the Moderate pricing season, your whole stay is charged at the Value price).

This can work either to your benefit or not as your arrival date could be in the High Season and your other nights in the Regular Season. In this case, you will pay the High Season rate for the entire duration.

There are two solutions: change your dates, or book one package for the more expensive night(s) and then another separate package for the cheaper remaining night(s).

If you book two back-to-back stays, ask the *Cast Member* checking you in whether you can keep the same room.

To see what season you will arrive in, use the live booking function on disneylandparis.com.

A booking agent can advise you of the best option if you book over the phone.

More on Pricing

Room prices in this section are based on arrivals from 1 April 2025 to 30 March 2026.

Prices listed include park tickets for all days of your stay, including check-in and check-out days.

Prices are per room per night for a standard room based on two adults sharing. Additional adults after the second pay a nightly surcharge.

Children under 3 always stay free; children 3 to 11 pay a child price, but there are often sales where the fee is waived for kids.

Multiple-night stays carry a lower "per night" cost. The per-night price after the third night is 45% to 85% cheaper, as most visitors will not need more than four days to visit the resort. This can make an extended stay at the hotels much better value for money overall.

MagicPass:

The *MagicPass* is exclusive to the seven Disneyland Paris-operated hotels and is given to you at check-in.

It allows you to enter the theme parks, including during *Extra Magic Time*, access the hotel pools, and park for free both at the hotel and the theme park parking lot. Plus, it acts as your room key and stores meal plan credits.

During check-in, you can also link a credit or debit card to your *MagicPass*, allowing you to pay for food and merchandise at most resort locations using the *MagicPass* instead of paying with your credit card or in cash each time. You then settle the bill when checking out and pay one lump sum.

Payment card linking can be a good option for guests from non-Euro countries whose banks charge a per-transaction foreign currency fee. Just be sure to monitor your spending to stay within budget.

NEW: An optional digital version of the *MagicPass* is now part of the Disneyland Paris app. This allows you to use mobile check-in to skip visiting the front desk and head to the parks. You can also view your park tickets, access Guest parking and use your Meal Plan vouchers. You can even use your phone as a room key at select resorts (*Disneyland Hotel* and *Hotel New York*).

Note: Some small stalls (such as those selling drinks or popcorn) do not accept *MagicPass* or credit/debit cards and only take cash. Disney does not operate most restaurants in *Disney Village*, so most of these also do *not accept the MagicPass* – but do ask.

How to book your stay:

We recommend booking Disneyland Paris hotels or packages through the official website at www.disneylandparis.com.

The website offers you several room types, but suites must be booked over the phone.

Disneyland Paris regularly runs promotions with discounts off the regular price, or 'get free nights' deals when you book a stay.

Offers vary seasonally and between different countries. These can be anything from 'free hotel, park tickets and transport for under 12s' to 'free half board meal plans' or even 40% or 50% off a stay. A minimum stay of two or three nights usually applies to promotions, as well as date restrictions.

Booking Tips

Tip 1: You can pay in instalments instead of one lump sum, with no interest. This allows you to modify your reservation up until you have paid the full amount. So, if a better offer becomes available after you book, you can make changes until the final balance is paid, such as upgrading your hotel or adding meal vouchers.

Tip 2: Disneyland Paris runs different promotions in different areas of Europe at the same time. The good news is you can book any promotion from any country. Visit www.disneylandparis.com - at the top of the page, select another country and then try booking there. You will pay in the local currency of that country. The website's language may also change when you do this. You can also do this by calling Disneyland Paris directly and stating the specific offer you would like to book.

Disneyland Hotel

This 5-star, 469-room, 18-suite, Art Deco/Victorian Hotel is the height of luxury at Disneyland Paris. It is located right at the entrance of Disneyland Park and is only 3 minutes from Walt Disney Studios Park.

The Disneyland Hotel is the most expensive and luxurious place to stay at Disneyland Paris. In 2024, the hotel reopened after a radical transformation.

The hotel offers a mix of regular and deluxe rooms, and signature suites, with views over *Fantasia Gardens* and even *Disneyland Park*.

As well as the regular rooms, 41 *Castle Club* rooms are sold as a "hotel-within-a-hotel". The *Castle Club* offers a lounge area with complimentary non-alcoholic beverages during the day and a perfect view of the fireworks through the windows at night. At *Castle Club*, princess characters appear in the morning. There is even a private lift directly to the turnstiles without walking through the rest of the hotel. This is a truly unique, premium experience.

The *Disneyland Hotel Spa by Clarins* offers facials, body treatments and massages.

A *My Royal Dream*

experience is available, including for non-hotel guests. Here guests get a makeover with costumes, accessories and more. Packages range from €95 to €440 per person including a photoshoot and a framed souvenir photo, makeup, hairstyling and more. Available for all ages. Book at the Disneyland Paris app up to 1 month in advance.

Room Size: Up to 40.7m² for standard rooms (up to 4 people, plus one child under 3 years old in a cot), and 42m² in the *Castle Club*. Other suites go up to 206m² – there are Sleeping Beauty, Cinderella, Frozen, Rapunzel and Beauty and the Beast

signature suites with the largest being the *Beauty and the Beast Princely Suite* and the *Royal Frozen Suite*.

Breakfast: Extra charge. €45 per adult and €36 per child.

Standard Room Prices
1 night: €806 to €1430.
2 nights: €1421 to €3746.
3 nights: €2044 to €5432.
4 nights: €2645 to €7039.

Activities: An indoor pool with a separate kids paddling pool, sun deck and fitness suite. The Royal Kids Club offers interactive fun.

Extras: A pillow menu with 7 pillow types. Character happenings at the hotel.

Dining

Royal Banquet (€€€€€) [PRMP] – Buffet Service. Dine with Disney characters at lunch and dinner. Pricing is €100 per adult and €50 per child.
La Table de Lumière (€€€€€) [PRMP] – Table Service. Dinner only. This elevated fine dining experience is the most luxurious in all of Disneyland Paris. As well as an elegant, gourmet atmosphere, guests will be able to meet and take photos with a royal Disney character couple such as Belle and her Prince, Aurora and Philip, or Tiana and Naveen. A 3-course set menu is €120 per adult or €60 per child.
Fleur de Lys Bar – Hotel Bar, serving drinks and snacks. Serves cocktails, champagne, other wines, soft drinks & hot drinks. Expect to pay €10 for coffees and €25 for cocktails.

Disney's Hotel New York - The Art of Marvel

This 4-star, Art Deco, New York-themed hotel features 565 rooms and 27 suites, and is a mere 10-minute walk to the parks. A shuttle bus is also available.

Themed to an apartment block in the Big Apple, this is the second closest hotel to the parks, and is located by the entrance of *Disney Village* and *Lake Disney*.

The hotel has a Marvel theme throughout, including over 350 pieces of art by over 110 artists.

Room Size: 31m² in standard rooms (for 4 people). *Empire State Club* lodging includes Club Rooms and Club Suites (56m² to 166m²).

Breakfast: Extra charge. €32 per adult and €26 per child.

Standard Room Prices:
1 night: €510 to €922
2 nights: €828 to €2296
3 nights: €1154 to €3257
4 nights: €1460 to €4139.

Empire State Club rooms are €70 to €416 extra per night.

Activities: Heated outdoor and indoor pools, adults-only steam rooms, tennis courts and a gym. Massages are available for a fee. Hotel guests only can access *Marvel Superhero Photo Spots* and meet Spider-Man, as well as enjoy the *Marvel Design Studio* kids area.

Extras: Dry cleaning is available. Suites and *Empire State Club* rooms are also available in addition to standard rooms - breakfast is included in these Club-level rooms. Suites are themed to Avengers, Super Hero and Spider-Man.

Dining
Manhattan Restaurant (€€€€€) [PLMP] – Offers an Italian menu. Dine under the "Chandelier of Asgard". Dinner only.
Downtown Restaurant (€€€€€) [PLMP] – Serves Chinese, American and Italian cuisine. Also serves breakfast.
Skyline Bar – Enjoy simulated "top of a skyscraper" views as Iron Man zips by.
Bleecker St. Lounge – A hip loft-style hangout.

Disney's Newport Bay Club

This 4-star, New England-style hotel features 1093 rooms and 13 suites. It is a 15-minute walk to the parks, or a free shuttle bus journey away.

Themed to New England, this nautical-inspired hotel houses two restaurants and anchors one end of Lake Disney. It is the fourth closest hotel to the parks.

It is one of our favourite hotels in terms of design but it can often feel a bit overwhelming with its huge size.

Room Size: Standard rooms are 27m²; family rooms for up to 6 guests are also available. Suites include the Admiral's Floor at 27m², Honeymoon Suites from 50m² to 63m², The Resort Suite at 55m² and the Presidential Suite measuring 84m².

Breakfast: Extra charge. €30 per day per adult and €24 per child.

Guests staying in *Compass Club* (club level) rooms have access to a complimentary breakfast.

Standard Room Prices:
1 night: €415 to €728
2 nights: €638 to €1870
3 nights: €870 to €2605
4 nights: €1080 to €3254.

For *Compass Club* rooms, add an extra €125 to €265 per night.

Activities: Indoor and outdoor pool, with deckchairs; sauna/steam bath and a gym. There is an indoor kids' play area.

Extras: This hotel has a convention centre. Dry cleaning is available at a surcharge.

Dining
Yacht Club (€€€€€) [PLMP] – Table Service. Serves New England specialities with Mediterranean influences.
Cape Cod (€€€€) [PLMP] – Buffet. Serves breakfast, lunch and dinner.
Captain's Quarters – Hotel Bar, serving drinks and snacks.

Disney's Sequoia Lodge

Recreating the ambience of the American National Parks, the 3-star Sequoia Lodge's 1011 rooms and 14 suites are a 15-minute walk from the parks. A shuttle is also available.

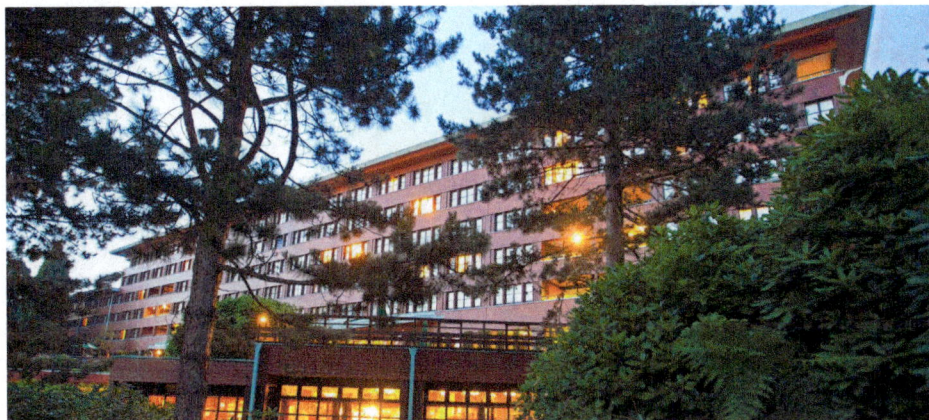

Disney's Sequoia Lodge is our favourite on-site hotel in terms of value for money.

It is a mid-priced hotel but is slightly closer to the parks than the pricier *Newport Bay Club Hotel*.

This hotel is one of the best themed on property with a fantastic lounge and pool.

This hotel is due to undergo a phased refurbishment soon. Exact dates have not been announced.

Room Size: 22m² in a standard room. *Golden Forest Club* rooms (club level with a private lounge with snacks) are also available, as are

Honeymoon Suites and Hospitality Suites (55m²).

Breakfast: Extra charge. €30 per day per adult and €24 per child. Breakfast is included in *Golden Forest Club* rooms.

Standard Room Prices:
1 night: €393 to €647
2 nights: €543 to €1514
3 nights: €727 to €2085
4 nights: €891 to €2576.

Golden Forest Club rooms are an extra €125 to €195 per room per night.

Activities: Indoor and outdoor pool, a gym, and sauna/steam bath. Massages are available for an extra charge. Kids' play areas are also available.

Dining
Hunter's Grill and Beaver Creek Tavern (€€€€) [BRMP] – Buffet in a rustic lodge-like setting.
Redwood Bar and Lounge – This amazing Hotel Bar and Lounge is undoubtedly one of our favourites. You can't help but feel you are in the middle of the American wilderness with the huge fireplace and cosy chairs. It is the perfect stop during winter evenings.

Disney's Hotel Cheyenne

Themed to America's Old Wild West, with details from the Toy Story films, this 1000-room, 3-star hotel is a 20-minute walk from the parks. A shuttle is also available.

Disney's Hotel Cheyenne is one of Disneyland Paris' more affordable onsite official Disneyland Paris hotels.

The rooms and services offered are more basic than the previously mentioned hotels. For example, you won't have access to a pool or gym, but you still have access to *Extra Magic Time* (early theme park entry), and you can walk to the theme parks (or get a complimentary shuttle bus).

In terms of overall theming, this is one of the most well-themed hotels, with the buildings shaped to look like they are part of the Wild West. It is also one star rating higher than the *Santa Fe* (see the next page) but is very similarly priced.

Room Size: Standard rooms measure 21m².

Breakfast: Extra charge. €25 per day per adult and €20 per child.

Standard Room Prices:
1 night: €367 to €647
2 nights: €543 to €1514
3 nights: €727 to €2085
4 nights: €891 to €2576.

Activities: Video games room; outdoor and indoor kids play areas; seasonal pony rides are available for an extra charge.

Dining
Chuck Wagon Café (€€€€) [PLMP] – Buffet. A continental breakfast is available. Dinner is a buffet.
Red Garter Saloon – Hotel Bar, serving snacks and drinks.
Starbucks (€) – Snacks, sandwiches and coffees from the world-famous chain.

Disney's Hotel Santa Fe

Themed to Santa Fe, in South West America, and with nods to Pixar's 'Cars' films. This 2-star, 1000-room hotel is a 20-minute walk from the parks. A shuttle is also available.

Disney's Santa Fe is the most affordable way to stay at an official Disneyland Paris hotel. It is the only 2-star hotel at the resort.

The rooms and services on offer are more basic than the other hotels. For example, you won't have access to a pool or gym, but you still have Wi-Fi, access to *Extra Magic Time* (early theme park entry), and you can walk to the theme parks or get a complimentary shuttle bus. Please note this hotel is the only official Disneyland Paris hotel NOT to have air conditioning.

In terms of theming, this is our least favourite hotel - the buildings do resemble some in real Santa Fe, but it is not the most magical of themes. This hotel is usually slightly cheaper than *Disney's Hotel Cheyenne,* but not always.

This hotel is also marginally further away from the theme parks than *Disney's Hotel Cheyenne*, making it the furthest from the parks. Despite that, it is still much more convenient than any non-official hotel, and the rooms have fun *Cars*-themed touches which kids will love.

Room Size: A standard room measures 21m² (sleeps up to 4 people plus 1 child under 3 years in a cot). Family rooms for up to 6 people are also available.

Breakfast: Extra charge. €22 per day per adult and €18 per child.

Standard Room Prices:
1 night: €337 to €570
2 nights: €482 to €1296
3 nights: €636 to €1759
4 nights: €768 to €2141.

Activities: A video game arcade is available.

Dining
La Cantina (€€€) [STMP] – Dinner buffet from 6:00pm to 10:30pm. A continental breakfast is also available.
Rio Grande Bar – Hotel Bar.
Starbucks Coffee (€) – Snacks, sandwiches and coffees from the world-famous chain.

Disney's Davy Crockett Ranch

Unlike the other Disney accommodation, Davy Crockett Ranch is not a hotel, but a 595-cabin campsite. It is rated as 3-star accommodation.

At *Disney's Davy Crockett Ranch*, you do not stay in a hotel room, but a large log cabin instead. Each cabin is private to you and your party only and features an outdoor area with tables and chairs.

You truly do feel a world away from the theme parks in a serene environment. This accommodation is ideal for large groups with rooms for up to 6 people.

Davy Crockett Ranch is not located near any of the other on-site hotels. It is also further than most of the partner hotels as it is an 8km (15-minute) drive to the theme parks - you will need your own transport as shuttle buses are not available.

Note that daily cleaning of cabins is an extra charge. In 2025, Disneyland Paris is swapping out cabins for more modern versions. This should not affect your stay.

Room Size: There are both 1-bedroom (36m^2) and 2-bedroom (39m^2) cabins available. Cabins sleep up to 6 people. A Premium 2-bedroom cabin option is also available.

Breakfast: Extra charge - €14 per person (all ages).

Standard Cabin Prices:
1 night: €333 to €566
2 nights: €475 to €1287
3 nights: €624 to €1744
4 nights: €753 to €2121.

Activities: There is a beautiful heated indoor swimming pool at this resort, as well as tennis

courts, a video games arcade, pony rides, quad bikes, indoor and outdoor children's play areas, a small farm and an adventure ropes course nearby *(Davy's Crockett Adventure - see page 80)*. Some activities require a surcharge.

Dining
Davy Crockett's Tavern (€€€) [PLMP] – Buffet in a woodland tavern.
Crockett's Saloon – Hotel Bar.

Center Parcs Villages Nature Paris

Originally created in partnership between Pierre et Vacances and Disney. Disney has since sold its share and this is now operated by Center Parcs as a 4-star partner hotel.

This unique experience is not an official Disneyland Paris hotel - nor is this actually at Disneyland Paris. However, Disney sells room-and-ticket packages here, it is nearby and is a popular place to stay.

Center Parcs Villages Nature Paris is designed to be an example of sustainable living with guests staying in apartments surrounded by nature. The resort is built around a huge indoor waterpark called the *Aqualagon* where the water is heated by geothermal energy.

The resort is around a 15-minute drive from Disneyland Paris, or 25

minutes by public bus route (a small charge applies).

This accommodation is perfect for large groups with apartments for up to 6 people.

Room Size: There are 1-bedroom (44m^2), 2-bedroom (52m^2) and 3-bedroom (65m^2) apartments available. These sleep up to 6 people. Premium cabins are also available.

Standard 1-Bedroom Prices:
1 night: €366 to €630
2 nights: €506 to €1287
3 nights: €698 to €1643
4 nights: €853 to €2017.

Please note that the accommodation prices quoted for 3 and 4-night

stays only include tickets for 2 days.

Activities: Indoor waterpark and outdoor geothermal lagoon, an escape room, "extraordinary gardens" to explore, pony club, indoor play area, outdoor play area, lake beach (swimming in summer only), aerial obstacle trails (extra charge), fitness trail, spa, bowling alley, and bike rentals.

Extras: A bakery, mini-market, and farmers market. Bars and restaurants on-site. Laundry facilities are available.

Dining
Aqualagon Café – Refreshments, snacks and treats.
Bowling Alley Bar – Hotel Bar.
Lakeside Promenade – Many options from counter service to quick service, bistro to a wine bar, and healthy meals to gourmet delicacies.

Partner and Nearby Hotels

Partner hotels are located just outside the main Disneyland Paris area. These are often much more affordable than Disney's hotels. You can also book these hotels independently without park tickets. We have also included other nearby (not partner) hotels. Prices are typically €200-€300 per person per night (based on 2 adults per room).

Hotel l'Elysée - Val d'Europe (Partner Hotel) [4*]
Number of Rooms: 152 rooms, including 4 executive suites.
Room Size: Cosy rooms (24m² - 2 person limit), family rooms (24m² - 4 person limit), family XL rooms (up to 48m² - 8 person limit) and exec suites (38m² - 4 person limit).
Breakfast: Included in most rates.
Activities: None.
Extras: Free Wi-Fi is available throughout the hotel, including in guest rooms. Meeting rooms are available. Laundry is available for an additional charge. 1-minute walk to *Val d'Europe* RER train station.
Dining: *Le George* – Table Service (lunch only); and *Le Diplomate* – Bar.

Staycity Aparthotels Paris, Marne La Vallée (Partner Hotel) [4*]
Number of Rooms: 284 rooms
Room Size: Studios (26m², sleeps 3), Family Studio (27m², sleeps 4), 1 Bedroom Apartment (31m², sleeps 4), Family Apartment (38m², sleeps 5). Also has a 5-Bed Villa, sleeping 16.
Breakfast: Self-catering in most rates.
Activities: Outdoor heated swimming pool, fitness centre, video game arcade.
Extras: Free Wi-Fi throughout the hotel, including in rooms.
Dining: Self-catering kitchenettes in all rooms. A breakfast buffet is available, as well as a bar serving cold drinks, pizzas, sandwiches and snacks.

Ki Space Hotel & Spa (Partner Hotel) [4*]
Number of Rooms: 274 rooms and suites.
Room Size: Double rooms (27-30m²), family rooms (30-34m²), junior suites (44m²), deluxe suites (85m²). Connecting suites are also available, up to 144m² and sleeping up to 12 people.
Breakfast: Not included in most rates.
Activities: Heated indoor swimming pool and jacuzzi, gym, video game arcade, and spa (extra charge)
Extras: Free Wi-Fi is available throughout the hotel, including in guest rooms. Note this hotel is further than the other hotels by shuttle - 20 minutes to the parks instead of 10 minutes.
Dining: *Nomad Restaurant* – Buffet; and *Bar-lounge* – including a robot bar. Rooms also all have a kitchenette.

ApartHotel Adagio Val d'Europe (Partner Hotel) [Aparthotel]
Number of Rooms: 290 rooms and suites.
Room Size: Studios (21m²), 1 to 3 bedroom apartments (27m² to 53m²)
Breakfast: Included in most rates.
Activities: Swimming pool.
Extras: Free Wi-Fi throughout the hotel, including in rooms.
Dining: There is no restaurant (except the buffet breakfast room). Guest rooms include kitchenettes to cook meals.

B&B Hotel (Partner Hotel) [2*]

Number of Rooms: 400 rooms.
Room Size: Standard rooms measure 15m^2 for up to 5 people.
Breakfast: Included in most rates.
Activities: Carousel and video games room.
Extras: Free Wi-Fi is available throughout the hotel, including in guest rooms.
Dining: Breakfast – Buffet; *Les Halles* - Snack Bar; and *BAR* - Bar.

Campanile Val de France (Not a Partner Hotel) [3*]

Number of Rooms: 300 rooms.
Room Size: Standard rooms measure 18.5m^2 for up to 4 people.
Breakfast: Included in most rates.
Activities: Carousel, video games room, and indoor children's play area.
Extras: Free Wi-Fi is available throughout the hotel, including in guest rooms.
Dining: *Le Marché Gourmand* – Buffet; and *L'Abreuvoir* – Bar.

Explorers Fabulous Hotels Group (Partner Hotel) [3*]

Number of Rooms: 390 rooms.
Room Size: Standard crew rooms measure 18m^2 to 22m^2.
Breakfast: Included in most rates.
Activities: Swimming pool, play areas, video games room, and kids fitness area.
Extras: Free Wi-Fi is available throughout the hotel including in guest rooms. Themed suites are also available.
Dining: *La Plantation* – Buffet; *Captain's Library* – Table Service; *Marco's Pizza* – Quick Service; and *Smuggler's Tavern and Trader's Cafe Bar* – Bar

More about Partner Hotels

Partner Hotels have no Disney theming, but they are kid-friendly and the staff have *some* knowledge of the theme parks. All these hotels provide frequent shuttle buses, with journeys taking 7-20 minutes depending on the hotel. Wait times for buses may be up to 30 minutes in the low season; buses run every 10 to 15 minutes at peak times.

Most of the hotels also have a Disney shop where in-park purchases can be delivered. Partner hotels do not generally include city taxes when booked – these must be paid at check-in and are about €1-€2 per adult per night. If you don't wish to book a package with tickets, use a hotel aggregator such as Hotels.com or Booking.com to compare prices. For packages, book directly at DisneylandParis.com

Tickets

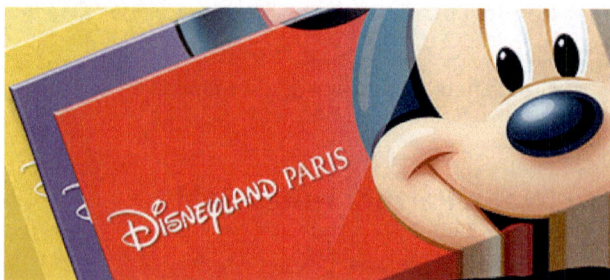

Important: If you have booked a Disney hotel, you can skip this section, as park tickets are included in your package unless you specifically make a room-only reservation.

At the Park

It is not possible to buy tickets at the entrance to the theme parks with the exception of discounted tickets for disabled guests at Guest Services (these are 25% off and require proof of disability - they can also be purchased online).

Online

Ticket prices at Disneyland Paris vary depending on the date of your visit and the visit length. The guide to the right will give you an idea of pricing but you can check the exact price of your ticket at disneylandparis.com.

If you opt to have the tickets posted to your home address, the tickets must be purchased at least 8 days before the date of your visit (additional charges apply). Alternatively, you can simply print them off straight away or add them to the Disneyland Paris app.

2-Park tickets allow you to visit both parks on the same day. Discounted single-day tickets bought online can be purchased up to one day before the date of your visit. They cannot be used on the day of purchase unless you buy a full-priced "undated" ticket online (see right). You must choose the date of your visit in advance to enjoy the lower rates.

Tickets can be cancelled for free up to 72 hours before visits. Seasonal pricing means that tickets can get more expensive closer to the date, so if you know when you are visiting, grab your ticket up to 16 months in advance.

> If you choose to buy an undated ticket, you must register it before entering the park. Tickets booked for specific dates or included in a hotel package are registered without you having to do anything.
>
> If you have purchased an undated ticket, you must register to enter the theme parks at www.disneylandparis.com/en-gb/register-tickets/.

Online Ticket Prices
1 day/1 park
Adult: €51-107;
Child: €47-100

1 day/2 parks
Adult: €76-132;
Child: €72-125

2 days/2 parks
Adult: €132-256;
Child: €124-242

3 days/2 parks
Adult: €193-381;
Child: €183-360

4 days/2 parks
Adult: €255-461;
Child: €240-436

Undated Tickets
Adult: 1 Park - €119,
2 Parks - €144
Child: 1 Park - €111,
2 Parks - €136

Children are 3 to 11 year olds. Under 3s enter for free — proof of age may be requested.

Prices fluctuate based on demand. Special prices apply for tickets for the 14 July, 31 October and 31 December. Expect to pay up to €175 per person for these days.

Disneyland Pass - Annual Pass

The 'Disneyland Pass' gives you a year of benefits for the price of a few days' entry. Passes are available to all visitors from any country. You must book the dates of your visit in advance online - guests can book 3 dates at any one time.

Bronze: €289	Silver: €499	Gold: €699
Access to the parks 170 days per year. *For a first visit of 2 consecutive days, day 2 registration is only possible once you have entered the parks on day 1 (subject to availability).*	Access to the parks 300 days per year.	Access to the parks 365 days per year.
Unlimited parking is included.	Unlimited parking is included.	Unlimited parking is included.
	Shops: 10% discount	Shops: 15% discount
	Dining: 10% discount	Dining: 15% discount
	10% off a year of *Photopass+*	1-Year *PhotoPass+* included
		Access to Extra Magic Time.

How do I buy an annual pass?
You can buy the annual pass at the Disneyland Pass ticket office outside the theme park, over the phone or online (via the French, Dutch or Belgian websites). You can pay all in one go, or in monthly instalments. If you buy your Disneyland Pass at the theme park, it will be valid from the day of purchase. If you buy your Disneyland Pass over the phone, a voucher will be sent to you by post. This voucher will need to be exchanged on your first visit, for your permanent Disneyland Pass at the park entrance. This voucher must be exchanged within 2 months of purchase. If you buy your Disneyland Pass online, it will become valid the day after the purchase.

Should I get an annual pass?
If you are visiting for four days or longer, consider getting an annual pass as it gives you discounts on food, merchandise and more. One pass can get you discounts for up to 6 people. An annual pass also makes sense if you are planning to return within a year. An annual pass even makes sense on shorter trips if you are a big foodie or love shopping for merchandise.

Blackout Dates

Bronze Pass:
December 2024: Every weekend, and 23-31
January 2025: 1-5
February 2025: 15-28
March 2025: Every weekend except 2 March
April 2025: 5-30
May 2025: 1-4, 8-11, 17-18, 24, 25, 29-31
June 2025: Every weekend and also 9 June
July 2025: 5-31
August 2025: Every day
September 2025: 1-2, and every weekend

Silver Pass:
December 2024: 21-31
January 2025: 1-5
February 2025: None
March 2025: None
April 2025: 19-27
May 2025: 1-4, 8-11, 29-31
June 2025: 1, 7-9
July 2025: None
August 2025: None
September 2025: None

Blackout dates are days when your pass does not allow you entry into the parks. Blackout dates had not been released beyond September 2025 at the time of publishing.

The Disneyland Pass does not grant access to the theme parks during special events, party evenings, or when the Disney Parks are closed due to exceptional circumstances.

Understanding the Parks

Before taking a detailed look at each of the theme parks, let us explain some of the must-knows, including parking, Disney Premier Access, character meets and much more.

Disney Premier Access

Disneyland Paris offers a paid skip-the-queue system called *Disney Premier Access*. If you use it, you can skip the regular queue and ride within minutes via a dedicated entrance.

How do I use it?

The easiest way to use the system is to use the official Disneyland Paris app.

• **Step 1:** Download the official Disneyland Paris App and log in or create an account. Link your park tickets or hotel reservation.

• **Step 2:** When in the park, choose an attraction you would like to use *Disney Premier Access* on. Not all attractions are available.

• **Step 3:** You will be given a 1-hour time slot to return at - this will be the earliest available time. You cannot manually choose a different time slot. If this time slot is convenient for you, pay for your *Disney Premier Access*.

• **Step 4:** While waiting for your time slot, you can do something else such as shop, dine, watch a show or experience another attraction using the standby queue line.

• **Step 5:** Return at the selected time and enter via the dedicated *Disney*

Premier Access ride entrance. Scan your QR code from the app and you'll be riding in minutes.

Do I need a smartphone?

If you don't have a smartphone, or don't want to use it, then you can purchase *Disney Premier Access* at Guest Services in either park.

How much does Disney Premier Access cost?

Price varies based on the attraction and how busy the park is. Each *Disney Premier Access* costs between €5 and €18 per person for one ride. It certainly isn't cheap!

What if the ride is having technical difficulties during my time slot?

A new QR code will be sent to you automatically at the end of your slot, or speak to a *Cast Member* at the ride entrance who can help you.

You can wait to see if the attraction re-opens or use

your new Pass to access the *Disney Premier Access* line for any other eligible attraction, at any time (no time slot).

Which attractions feature Disney Premier Access?

• *Autopia*
• *Avengers Assemble: Flight Force*
• *Big Thunder Mountain*
• *Buzz Lightyear Laser Blast*
• *Cars ROAD TRIP*
• *Crush's Coaster*
• *Indiana Jones et le Temple du Péril*
• *"it's a small world"*
• *Orbitron: Machines Volantes*
• *Peter Pan's Flight*
• *Phantom Manor*
• *Pirates of the Caribbean*
• *Ratatouille: The Adventure*
• *Spider-Man W.E.B. Adventure*
• *Star Tours: The Adventures Continue*
• *Star Wars Hyperspace Mountain*
• *The Twilight Zone Tower of Terror*

Will this really save me time?

Yes, due to the high price point, only a small percentage of visitors use it. So, you can expect to gain near-instant access using *Disney Premier Access*. During less busy periods, it is probably not worth it.

Do children need Disney Premier Access to join the dedicated line?

Children under three do not need a *Disney Premier Access* to join the dedicated queue line. They must, however, be accompanied by an adult who has *Disney Premier Access*. All other children and adults each need *Disney Premier Access*.

Can I buy as many Disney Premier Access as I want?

You may buy a maximum of 3 *Disney Premier Access* for each attraction per guest per day, and up to 12 *Disney Premier Access* per attraction and time slot at a time.

There are a limited number of *Disney Premier Access* available for each time slot.

What happened to Fastpass?

If you have previously visited Disneyland Paris and used the free *Fastpass* system, this is gone. Only the paid-for *Disney Premier Access* is available.

Are there any other options?

Yes, *Disney Premier Access* has two versions - *Disney Premier Access One* (operates as discussed on these last 2 pages), and *Disney Premier Access Ultimate* (€90-190) - this allows you to buy access to all eligible *DPA* attractions (except *Orbitron*) in one bundle with the added benefit of being able to enter at any time instead of only during designated time slots. Both versions only include use per attraction.

On-Ride Photos

Some of Disneyland Paris' most popular rides have cameras positioned and timed to take perfect on-ride photos of you at the most action-filled moments on attractions. Buy the photo and see yourself at the ride's fastest, steepest, scariest and most fun moment. These make for timeless keepsakes.

When you exit selected rides, you will walk past screens that preview your photo (with a watermark on top). If you wish to purchase it, go to the photo counter.

You do not have to buy on-ride photos straight after your ride; you can pick them up anytime that same day. Just remember your unique number at the ride exit, ask a member of staff at the photo kiosk to write it down or take a photo of your number.

If you like the photo, *Cast Members* will show it to you up close before you pay for it. If you like it, buy it! You will treasure the photo for a long time.

At some attractions, you can do this whole process yourself on a digital kiosk without needing to speak to a Cast Member.

Photo print prices start at €20 for one photo with a themed frame. A single photo without a frame is €15, and each additional photo costs €9. Digital photos cost the same as prints.

The attractions with on-ride photos are:
• *Big Thunder Mountain*
• *Pirates of the Caribbean*
• *Star Wars Hyperspace Mountain*
• *Buzz Lightyear Laser Blast*
• *The Twilight Zone: Tower of Terror.*
• *Avengers Assemble: Flight Force*

Top Tip: If you want photos from several rides, you can combine these on a *PhotoPass*. See our *PhotoPass* section on the following page to learn how to save money on photos.

Disneyland Paris App

Disneyland Paris has a free iOS and Android app, which allows you to enhance your trip. With the app, you can plan your stay, including an overview of the hotels and different attractions on offer. You can also create an itinerary and buy park tickets, as well as make restaurant reservations.

You can check the opening hours, see the timings of shows and parades, and check the attraction wait times. It is this last feature that makes the app the most useful. You can check waits in the palm of your hand for both parks at the same time.

Finally, the app allows you to pre-purchase/mobile order food and drink from some of the Quick Service restaurants, and buy *Disney Premier Access*.

NEW: An optional digital version of the *MagicPass* is now part of the Disneyland Paris app. This allows you to use mobile check-in to skip visiting the front desk before heading to the parks. You can also view your park tickets and Meal Plan vouchers. You can even use your phone as a room key at the *Disneyland Hotel* and *Hotel New York* and skip going to the check-in desk altogether.

You will need a data connection to see live information, which means you must have data access on your phone or you can use the free in-park Wi-Fi available to all guests.

Modern smartphones allow you to use a digital sim card (e-SIM) to access data when abroad and avoid roaming fees. Visit airalo.com and use coupon "GIOVAN9607" to get a $3 discount on all e-SIM plans so 3GB of data is $7, and 5GB is only $11.

PhotoPass

Disneyland Paris' *PhotoPass* is an easy-to-use system that makes collecting all your in-park photos easy.

You will find photographers dotted around the park. Simply go to any in-park photographer (including those stationed at *Meet Mickey Mouse*, *Princess Pavilion: A Royal Invitation*, and with other characters) and ask for a *Disney PhotoPass* after the photographer takes your photo.

Alternatively, you can ask for a *PhotoPass* card at any ride photo counter (this option is not advertised but is available if you ask).

Next time you have a photo taken, hand over your *PhotoPass* card and pictures will be added to it. You can do this throughout your visit and the photos will be kept together on the system. This card can be re-used throughout both parks anywhere you find a photographer or with on-ride photos.

Each photo is saved on the *PhotoPass* system for 7 days. Before your photos expire, visit one of these locations to view and purchase your photos: *New Century Notions: Flora's Unique Boutique* in Disneyland Park or *Walt Disney Studios Store* in Walt Disney Studios Park. You can also view the photos at the Disney shops at the on-site hotels.

You can purchase prints or digital versions of your *PhotoPass* photos at all these locations. Multiple *PhotoPass* cards can be combined onto one account too.

The more photos you purchase, the lower the 'price per photo.' You can also add an extra Disney touch with themed borders and details for free.

If you have used *PhotoPass* in the American parks, the Disneyland Paris system works similarly, but the prints are more reasonably priced at Disneyland Paris. However, there are fewer *PhotoPass* photographers at the parks in France.

PhotoPass+

Like the regular *PhotoPass* (covered on the previous page), *PhotoPass+* allows you to collect ride and character photos, as well as photos in front of some iconic park locations. The difference here is that you pre-pay for unlimited digital photos instead of paying for each print individually. *PhotoPass+* costs €85 at the park for photos and videos.

PhotoPass+ includes a *PhotoPass+* card and a lanyard to carry the card on. Plus, two mini cards are included, so that other members of your party can have their own card and easily add photos to the same account.

Guests can add an unlimited number of photos to their account for 10 days following their *PhotoPass+* activation.

To view photos, guests should create an online account at DisneyPhotoPass.eu.

www.disneyphotopass.eu

Guests can view their photos on the website and download them in high quality, as well as buy prints, photo books, calendars, gifts and more.

Photos stay on the website for 1 year from the date of activating the card, giving you plenty of time to download your favourite images.

PhotoPass+ at Disneyland Paris is very similar to the *Memory Maker* system in the US parks – but on a smaller scale with much fewer photographers.

Guests who pre-book PhotoPass+ as part of their stay pay a reduced rate. A *PhotoPass+* voucher is given at check-in and can be exchanged at any in-park shop selling *PhotoPass+*.

Top Tip: Annual Pass discounts are available. Annual pass holders get a *PhotoPass+* card valid for one year from the date of purchase instead of just 10 days, offering fantastic value for money. The top annual tier pass includes *PhotoPass+* any no extra cost.

Rider Switch

Rider Switch is a time-saving solution that allows guests to reduce waiting times throughout their visit when riding attractions with height restrictions.

A common issue at theme parks is when two adults want to ride a thrill ride but have a child who is not tall enough to ride.

The solution is *Disney's Rider Switch* service, which allows one person to queue up and ride while the other stays with the child.

When the first person reaches the end of the queue line, they ask for a *Rider Switch* pass. After riding, they give this pass to the second person.

The second person is then able to ride as soon as the first one returns. The second person is granted near-immediate access to the ride, bypassing the regular queue line.

Each person will experience the ride separately, but the second person will not need to wait to ride.

Each attraction implements the system slightly differently, so ask the *Cast Member* at each ride entrance for details.

To use this service, you do not need to have a child or baby present. You could use it to stay with an adult who does not wish to ride too, for example.

Single Rider

One of the best ways to significantly reduce your time waiting for attractions is to use the *Single Rider* queue instead of the regular standby queue. This is available at selected attractions at the resort.

The *Single Rider* queue fills free spaces on ride vehicles. For example, if a ride vehicle can seat 8 people and a group of 4 turns up, followed by a group of 3, then a Single Rider will fill the free space. This allows guests willing to ride with strangers to experience a shorter wait and fill a space. This system ultimately reduces waits for everyone. *Single Rider* queues may be closed when waits in that queue are too long, or when the theme park is not busy.

Single Rider Lines can be used by groups too, but each person in the group will be separated, and each person will ride in a different vehicle. Groups can, of course, wait for each other by the ride exit but will not ride together.

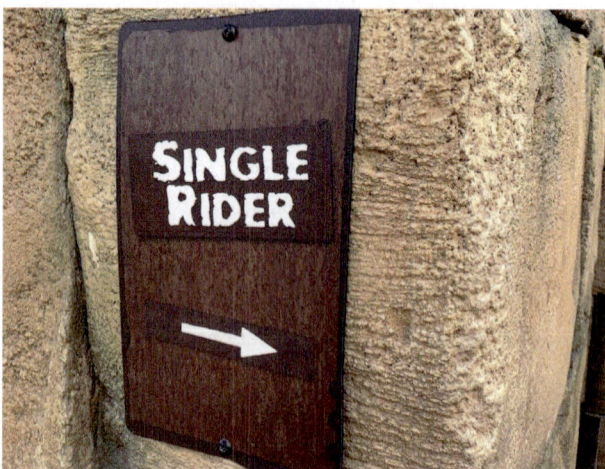

The following attractions operate Single Rider Lines:
• *RC Racer*
• *Toy Soldier Parachute Drop*
• *Crush's Coaster*
• *Ratatouille: The Adventure*
• *Star Wars Hyperspace Mountain*
• *Indiana Jones et le Temple du Péril*
• *Avengers Assemble: Flight Force*
• *Spider-Man W.E.B. Adventure*

Extra Magic Time

Extra Magic Time allows selected guests early theme park access to selected attractions at the theme parks at Disneyland Paris for 1 hour each morning.

Guests get access to an almost empty park, ride with little to no wait, and can often meet Disney characters too. Before the crowds arrive. *Extra Magic Time (EMT)* includes most major rides at both theme parks.

Extra Magic Time takes place at both theme parks daily from 8:30 am to 9:30 am. During less busy times of the year, only one of the two theme parks may be open for *EMT*. Check the Disneyland Paris calendar on the website for details.

Getting Extra Magic Time
The *EMT* benefit is available exclusively to guests staying at on-site Disney Hotels (not partner hotels) and for guests with a Gold Disneyland Pass (annual pass), even if they are not staying at a Disney hotel.

Disney hotel guests need their *MagicPass* (given at hotel check-in) to enter the parks during *Extra Magic Time*. Disneyland Pass holders need their pass.

What is open during EMT?
At Disneyland Park, selected attractions in *Discoveryland, Frontierland* and *Fantasyland* are available - that's every land except *Adventureland. Main Street, U.S.A.* is also open.

Typically, the following rides are available during *Extra Magic Time* – other rides and lands open at the official park opening time:
• *Dumbo: The Flying Elephant*
• *Peter Pan's Flight*
• *Lancelot's Carousel*
• *Mad Hatter's Teacups*
• *Les Voyages de Pinocchio*
• *Buzz Lightyear Laser Blast*
• *Star Tours: The Adventures Continue*
• *Hyperspace Mountain*
• *Orbitron*
• *Thunder Mesa Riverboat Landing*
• *Phantom Manor*
• *Big Thunder Mountain*.

Extra Magic Time at *Walt Disney Studios Park* typically includes the following attractions:
• *Crush's Coaster*
• *Spider-Man W.E.B. Adventure*
• *Avengers Assemble*
• *RC Racer*
• *Toy Soldiers Parachute Drop*
• *Slinky Dog Zig Zag Spin*
• *Flying Carpets Over Agrabah*
• *The Twilight Zone: Tower of Terror*
• *Ratatouille: The Adventure*.

Top Tip: As Disneyland Paris does not officially publish a list of rides that are open during *EMT*, the easiest way to find out is to open the Disneyland Paris app on the day of your visit - you can click on any ride on the map and its hours of operation will be published - if the time posted is before 9:30am, then that ride is open during EMT. You can also check in the days leading up to your visit to give you an idea of what you can expect to be open.

Wheelchair and Pushchair Rentals

Wheelchair and pushchair rentals are available for guests who do not wish to bring their own.

If your child is recently out of a pushchair, it is often still worth renting one as it is likely they will get tired, due to the large distances you will cover on foot during a Disneyland Paris trip.

Sometimes it is nice just to let kids sit in their pushchair and have a break. They can

also be used as an easy way to carry bags.

It should be noted that Disneyland Paris' pushchairs do not recline or have rain protection. Some people also say that the pushchairs are not the most comfortable so it may be worth bringing a cushion.

The daily cost of hiring a wheelchair or pushchair is €25. The deposit required for a wheelchair is €200; it is

€75 for a pushchair.

You are, of course, welcome to bring your own pushchair or wheelchair if you wish.

When experiencing attractions, you must leave your pushchair in the dedicated parking areas. Ask a *Cast Member* if you need clarification on these.

Cast Members may relocate pushchairs to keep them neat and organised.

Disney Shopping Service

The *Disney Shopping Service* allows you to buy an item at any of the theme park shops and pick it up later.

When paying for your goods before 3:00pm, ask to use the *Disney Shopping Service*. You will leave the item with the *Cast Member* who served you. When you have finished your day at the park, you can pick up your shopping. A minimum spend of €50 *may* apply.

You can either pick up your purchases at the W*orld of Disney* store in *Disney Village* from 6:00pm, or at the Disney boutiques at on-site Disney hotels or selected partner hotels from 8:00pm.

This means that you can collect all your items in one spot, even if you buy items from different shops.

This service allows you to be free to eat, shop, ride attractions and watch shows to your heart's content without carrying your shopping around.

NEW: Disneyland Paris has partnered with the *SkipTax* service and app to allow non-EU residents to reclaim VAT on purchases at the resort. Visit skiptax.com for more information.

Lockers

There are two staffed luggage services located to the right of each theme park's turnstiles.

There is also an external automatic left luggage storage facility on the upper level of *Marne-La-Vallee – Chessy* train station.

Storage at the parks and the station ranges from €5 to €15 depending on the size and the number of bags stored.

For the station lockers, you need the exact change (there is a change machine inside the locker room). At the Disney Parks storage facilities, you can pay by cash or by card.

You can access the Disneyland Paris storage as many times as you want throughout the day for one set daily fee. Do note, however, that queues are often long at the start and end of the day.

With the station lockers, every time you open the lockers, you must pay again to lock them. Plus, you must go through the Disneyland Paris security checkpoint (including airport-style bag scanners and metal detectors) each time to access the station lockers.

We recommend using the staffed lockers at the parks.

Larger Guests

Disneyland Paris has designed its attractions to be accessible to as many guests as possible. However, a visitor's height or weight may sometimes limit the attractions they can visit for safety reasons.

At Disneyland Paris, unlike some other theme parks, there are no 'test seats' outside attractions. Therefore, if you are unsure whether you will be able to ride a particular attraction, it is best to speak to a *Cast Member* at the ride entrance.

You could also ask the *Cast Member* whether they could allow you to try sitting in the ride vehicle itself before queuing up but this is not guaranteed.

Rides where larger guests may have difficulty include *Star Wars Hyperspace Mountain, Avengers Assemble: Flight Force, Indiana Jones et le Temple du Péril, Crush's Coaster* and *RC Racer* because of the safety restraints and limited legroom.

Orbitron and *Cars Quatre Roues Rallye* may also be a tight fit despite using seatbelt-style restraints.

Meeting the Disney Characters

For many visitors, meeting characters is the highlight of their trip. Playing with Pluto, talking to Cinderella and hugging Mickey makes for magical memories.

Disneyland Park:
Characters are scheduled to appear around the park throughout the day. Please note that characters may meet at different locations than those shown here.

Mickey is at *Meet Mickey Mouse* in *Fantasyland*, and the Disney princesses can be seen at *Princess Pavilion* (also in *Fantasyland*).

You will find Alice and her friends near *Alice's Curious Labyrinth*, including The Mad Hatter, Tweedle Dum, and Dee. Nearby at *The Old Mill* you'll often find Stitch.

On *Main Street, U.S.A.*, you can meet Winnie the Pooh and Friends. By *Casey's Corner,* you can see Chip and Dale.

Woody and Friends are often found by *Cowboy Cookout Restaurant*, and Baloo by *Hakuna Matata Restaurant* in *Adventureland*.

Elsewhere in *Adventureland*, you can expect to see Captain Hook and friends by *Pirate's Beach*, and Aladdin and friends near *Agrabah Café*.

At *Starport* in *Discoveryland*, you can meet Darth Vader or other Star Wars characters.

Details vary by season and date so check the Disneyland Paris app for the latest information.

If there is a specific character you would like to see, ask at *City Hall* (on *Town Square*) whether they have a schedule for them. Not all characters are available to meet daily.

You can also have a Disney Princess dining experience at *L'Auberge de Cendrillon* (€100 per adult, €50 per child).

Characters usually stop meeting in both parks around mid-afternoon.

Walt Disney Studios Park:
You will find many characters in the *Toon Studio* area of the park to the left of *Crush's Coaster* at permanent outdoor photo locations. Here you will often find Mickey, Minnie, Buzz Lightyear, Woody and other characters. Check the app for exact character appearances.

At *Animation Celebration*, you can meet Olaf from Frozen.

At *Hero Training Center* in *Avengers Campus*, you can meet Iron Man, Captain Marvel, another Avenger or even Spider-Man. This requires a reservation which must be booked on the Disneyland Paris app - details may change but at the moment slots are released at 10:00am and 2:00pm.

Hotels:
Characters are present at on-site hotels in the morning at breakfast time. Guests staying at the *Hotel New York - Art of Marvel* can also meet Spider-Man at a photo location there. Non-hotel guests may be able to access this subject to availability (you will have better luck at this by showing up in the afternoon).

Classic characters such as Mickey, Minnie, Tigger, Chip and Dale and Donald Duck are also present during the character meals at *Royal Banquet* restaurant in the *Disneyland Hotel*.

Meanwhile at *La Table de Lumière* at *Disneyland Hotel*, you can expect exquisite dining in the company of the Disney princesses. This 3-course set meal is priced at €120 per person, plus €60 for optional wine pairings.

How to Spend Less time Queuing

Disneyland Paris meticulously themes its queues to introduce an attraction's story before you ride. However, no one likes waiting, and we all want to get on a ride as quickly as possible. Visiting a theme park will always involve waiting, but in this chapter, we cover our top tips for minimising your time spent in queue lines.

1 - Eat outside of typical dining hours

At Disneyland Paris, whether you want to eat at a Table Service restaurant or a Quick Service meal, waiting for your food is part of the game. Have lunch before midday or after 3:00pm for much shorter waits. Have dinner before 7:00pm to reduce your wait times. A wait of 45 minutes or longer to order is relatively typical at peak times at Quick Service restaurants.

2 - Quick Service meal tricks

At Quick Service locations, cashiers often have two queues, and alternate between them – count how many groups (or families) are in front of you in the queue. There may be ten people in front of you in one queue line but only two families. The other queue line may have five people but from five different families. The queue with ten people will move more quickly with only two orders to process versus the other queue's five orders.

3 - On-site Disney Hotel guests

If you are staying at an on-site Disneyland Paris hotel or have an annual pass with this benefit, take advantage of *Extra Magic Time* to get entry into the theme parks one hour before regular guests do.

During this time, you can experience many of the park's attractions with minimal waits. See our *Extra Magic Time* section on page 33 for more details.

4 - Mobile Order Quick Service Food

The Disneyland Paris app allows you to preorder your Quick Service meal, pay for it in-app and collect it at a specific time. This is currently available at *Café Hyperion, Casey's Corner, Casa de Coco, Restaurant Hakuna Matata, Last Chance Café, Au Chalet de la Marionette,* and *Cowboy Cookout Barbecue.* We expect this to be rolled out to more Quick Service restaurants over time. This is a great time-saver and a must-do.

5 - Consider skipping the parades and fireworks

If you have already seen the parades, shows or fireworks on one day, use that time to experience rides - the wait times for rides are often much shorter during these big events.

If you have not seen the park's entertainment offerings before, we do *not* recommend you skip them. Parades and shows are only performed at set times of the day and most of these are just as much a part of the Disney theme park experience as the rides.

6 - Ride outdoor attractions while it rains

Outdoor attractions such as *Dumbo, Flying Carpets over Agrabah, Casey Junior, Storybook Canal Boats, Big Thunder Mountain, Indiana Jones et le Temple du Peril, Lancelot's Carousel* (outdoor queue)*, Slinky Dog Zigzag Spin, Toy Soldiers Parachute Drop* and *RC Racer* have much-reduced waits when it is raining. Yes, you may get wet while riding but the wait times *will* be shorter too - and you can always weather a rain jacket, of course.

Top Tip: Many guests return to the hotels when it rains, so many indoor rides may also have shorter queues during inclement weather.

7 - Choose when to visit carefully

Visit during an off-peak time if possible. If you are visiting on New Year's Day, expect to queue a lot longer than on a random Tuesday in the middle of January. Seasonal events such as Christmas and Halloween also draw bigger crowds.

Of course, weekends are busier than weekdays. See our 'When to Visit' section (page 5) to make the most of your time.

8 - Shop at the end of the day

Go shopping at the end of the day. Even when the park is 'officially' closed, the shops on *Main Street, U.S.A.* stay open up to an hour longer than the rest of the park. Alternatively, walk over to *Disney Village* in the evening, and go shopping there until later in the evening - these shops often close at midnight during peak times!

Additionally, on-site hotels and some partner hotels have a small Disney boutique inside them.

Do not waste your time during the day shopping, do it at strategic times and make the most of your time in the parks.

9 - Download the Official Disneyland Paris App

Disneyland Paris' app contains all kinds of information from the wait times for the rides, to the timings of parades, shows, character appearances, restaurant opening hours and more.

As such, you will not waste time crossing the park to find out that a character you saw earlier in the day has now left a particular location, or that a ride is closed for technical difficulties. Plus, you can book restaurant reservations and order meals ahead of time. You can even check in online and head straight to the parks without having to visit the hotels first.

Dining

There are a variety of places to eat at Disneyland Paris. Food options vary from sandwich and snack locations to Quick Service (fast food) places, character buffets, Table Service dining and even fine dining options. Eating can be as much a part of the experience as the attractions at Disneyland Paris.

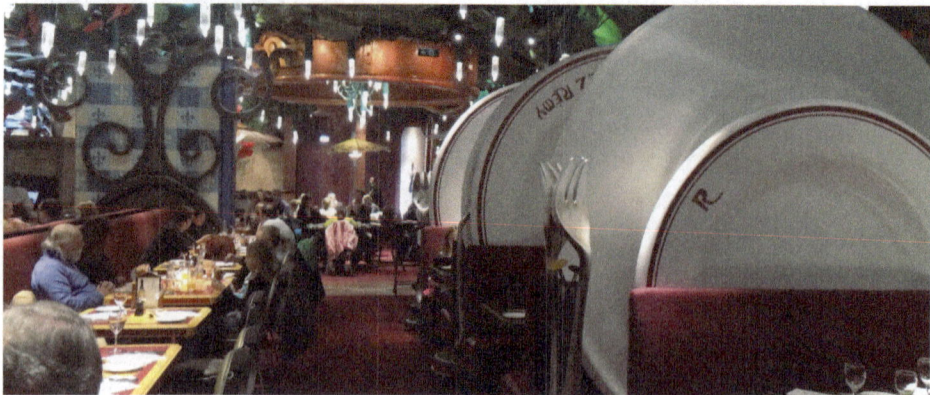

Making Reservations

If you want to guarantee you will be able to dine at a specific restaurant, we recommend booking a table in advance.

You can make your restaurant reservation up to 2 months in advance (or from the time of booking for Disney hotel guests) but, in reality, booking even two weeks or less beforehand will usually get you a table at *most* restaurants.

Most people do not book restaurants at Disneyland Paris far in advance, which is a stark difference from the American Disney parks.

Despite this, it is worth making a reservation as early as possible if you want a certain meal on a specific day. You will also be seated much more quickly with a reservation than without

one.

Purchasing a meal plan (see the next page) does not guarantee you a table in a restaurant, so be sure to make a restaurant reservation in advance if there is a particular place you want to dine.

The easiest way to make a reservation is to use the official Disneyland Paris app or website. You can browse all the restaurant menus and see pricing here.

Alternatively, you can call the Dining Reservation hotline on +33 (0)1 60 30 40 50 and book in several languages, including English.

You can also book at City Hall in Disneyland Park, Studio Services in Walt Disney Studios Park, or any of the Disney hotel lobbies.

Finally, you can visit any of the restaurants and book directly.

You do not need to stay at a Disney hotel to book a table at a restaurant - anyone visiting the theme parks can do this. If you cannot attend a reservation, it is good practice to cancel it as early as possible.

In the low season, it is possible to make reservations for the same day or the next day at most locations. In the high season, restaurants are fully booked a week or more in advance.

Top Tip: For *Auberge de Cendrillon*, it is worth booking as soon as reservations open - it is very popular. *Bistrot Chez Rémy* is also worth booking well in advance, as is *Walt's* and *Captain Jack's*.

Meal Plans

Meal Plans are pre-paid credits so that you do not need to worry about food costs when on your trip.

Meal Plan entitlements are digitally loaded onto your *MagicPass,* which is given when checking in at the hotel, as well as onto the Disneyland Paris app. Meal Plans are only available to guests booking packages with an official Disney Hotel and tickets.

All Half-Board Meal Plans include (per night):
• 1 Breakfast at your hotel
• 1 Table Service, Quick Service or Buffet meal

The Full-Board Standard Meal Plan includes (per night):
• Breakfast at your hotel
• 1 Quick Service meal
• 1 Table Service/Buffet meal
• 1 extra meal on the last day.

The Full-Board Plus Meal Plan includes (per night):
• Breakfast at your hotel
• 2 Quick Service, Table Service or Buffet meals
• 1 extra meal on the last day.

The Full-Board Extra Plus Meal Plan includes (per night):
• Breakfast at your hotel
• 2 Quick Service, Table Service or Buffet meals

• Use 1 of your Meal Plan Credits for a character dining meal
• 1 extra meal on the last day.

The Full-Board Premium Meal Plan includes (per night):
• Breakfast at your hotel
• 2 Quick Service, Table Service or Buffet meals
• Use your Meal Plan Credits at character dining meals (unlimited amount)
• 1 extra meal on the last day.

Standard, Plus and Extra Plus Meal Plans are valid at 35 restaurants at the resort. The Premium Meal Plan is valid at 38 restaurants.

A meal voucher includes a set menu or buffet, and one soft drink.

Occasionally, Disneyland Paris runs promotions with free Meal Plans included with package bookings.

If you eat at a restaurant not included in your Meal Plan, you can use your vouchers for a discount and pay the difference.

Pre-purchasing Meal Plans can save you money off the menu prices, although this depends on what you eat. Many guests choose Meal Plans for the peace of mind

of prepaying all their dining.

Meals are from a set menu on all Meal Plans - you do not get access to the full a la carte menu (also note no drinks are included in adult plans). At a buffet, all items are available (including one soft drink). If in doubt, ask your waiter before ordering.

The Half Board plans include one voucher per night for any restaurant from the grid on the next page; the Full Board plans include two vouchers per night for restaurants of your choice from the grid. Breakfast is also included in all plans. Breakfast is an extra charge for guests without meal plans.

Meal Plan vouchers are accepted at all Disney Park and Disney Hotel restaurants and in some *Disney Village* restaurants (not *McDonald's, Rainforest Cafe, Starbucks, Earl of Sandwich, Five Guys, The Royal Pub, Rosalie* and *Vapiano*).

Pricing:
The Meal plan prices below are per person per night.

For arrivals until March 2026

	Standard Adult	Standard Child	Plus Adult	Plus Child	Extra Plus Adult	Extra Plus Child	Premium Adult	Premium Child
Half Board	€55	€35	€65	€40	N/A	N/A	€135	€75
Full Board	€75	€45	€115	€60	€150	€80	€245	€135

The Standard Meal Plan is only available at *Disney's Davy Crockett Ranch* and *Hotel Santa Fe*. The Premium Meal Plan is only available for guests of the *Disneyland Hotel*. The Extra Plus Plan is *NOT* available to guests of the *Disneyland Hotel*.

Restaurant Name	Restaurant Type	Location	On **Standard/ Plus/Extra Plus Plan?**	On **Premium Plan?**
Agrabah Cafe	Buffet	Disneyland Park	Yes	Yes
Annette's Diner	Table Service	Disney Village	Yes	Yes
Auberge de Cendrillon	Character Dining	Disneyland Park	No	Yes
Beaver Creek Tavern	Table Service	Sequoia Lodge Hotel	Yes	Yes
Bistrot Chez Remy	Table Service	Walt Disney Studios Park	Yes	Yes
Cape Cod	Buffet	Newport Bay Club Hotel	Yes	Yes
Captain Jack's	Table Service	Disneyland Park	Yes	Yes
Chuck Wagon Cafe	Buffet	Hotel Cheyenne	Yes	Yes
Crockett's Tavern	Buffet	Davy Crockett's Ranch	Yes	Yes
Downtown Restaurant	Buffet	Disney's Hotel New York - Art of Marvel	Yes	Yes
Hunter's Grill	Buffet	Sequoia Lodge Hotel	Yes	Yes
La Cantina	Buffet	Santa Fe Hotel	Yes	Yes
La Table de Lumière	Character Dining	Disneyland Hotel	No	Yes
La Grange at Billy Bob's	Table Service	Disney Village	Yes	Yes
Plaza Gardens	Buffet	Disneyland Park	Yes	Yes
PYM Kitchen	Buffet	Walt Disney Studios Park	Yes	Yes
Royal Banquet	Character Buffet	Disneyland Hotel	No	Yes
Silver Spur Steakhouse	Table Service	Disneyland Park	Yes	Yes
The Lucky Nugget Saloon	Hybrid Service	Disneyland Park	Yes	Yes
The Steakhouse	Table Service	Disney Village	Yes	Yes
Walt's: An American Restaurant	Table Service	Disneyland Park	Yes	Yes
Yacht Club	Table Service	Newport Bay Club Hotel	Yes	Yes

Credits from all Meal Plans are also valid at all Quick Service restaurants at both theme parks.

Top Places to Eat

The Steakhouse - Located in *Disney Village*, this Table Service location has hands-down the best steaks on property. Delicious food and a great atmosphere make this a solid choice for any evening.

Bistrot Chez Rémy - This is the only Table Service option in *Walt Disney Studios Park*. The menu is limited, so do check it first, but if the food is to your liking, this is one of the best themed and most 'fun' restaurants at the resort.

The Lucky Nugget Saloon - Located in *Frontierland* in *Disneyland Park*. This restaurant has changed its dining concept several times. It is a Quick Service restaurant but the food is delivered to your table. Sometimes live shows play on the stage here too.

Restaurant Hakuna Matata Perhaps the best Quick Service location in Disneyland Paris with more unique options than your standard burgers and fries that are found throughout a

lot of the theme parks.

Plaza Gardens Restaurant - Our go-to option when we fancy a buffet. The selection is vast and the setting is great; with the right table, you may even be able to spy the park's iconic castle.

PYM Kitchen - Part of Walt Disney Studio Park's *Avenger's Campus*, this restaurant has a fun and unique variety of American-style buffet dishes.

Tipping in Restaurants

In France, a 15% service charge is included in your meal price, although this may not be itemised in the bill.

You are not expected to leave any additional money for service. French guests rarely leave a tip unless service is exceptional.

If you feel this is the case, feel free to leave a few Euros in cash. A 5% to 10% tip is enough.

Sometimes in France, waiters will not return with your change and assume it is their tip; if this was not your intention, let them know. This is less common at Disneyland Paris than elsewhere. One way to avoid this is to pay by card.

Good to Know

• For buffets, kids' prices apply for ages 3 to 11 inclusive.
• You may have the option of breakfast at *Plaza Gardens* or *Auberge de Cendrillon* in *Disneyland Park* for an extra charge.
• Adults can order from the kids' menu at Quick Service locations. At Table Service locations, this is at the discretion of the *Cast Member* serving you but is often not allowed.

• For an idea of how much meals cost at the restaurants, see our parks chapters which list price ranges.
• All restaurants should have at least one vegan option, but *Cast Members* and chefs will do their best to accommodate you. Making a reservation and stating your dietary requirements helps make this much easier for everyone.

Breakfast Pricing

Breakfast is not included with hotel reservations. Unless you purchase a Meal Plan or stay in a club-level suite, you will need to pay for breakfast separately.

These are the breakfast prices per person per night:
• **Davy Crockett Ranch** - €14 adult or child
• **Hotel Santa Fe** - €22 per adult, €18 per child
• **Hotel Cheyenne** - €25 per adult, €20 per child
• **Sequoia Lodge** - €30 per adult, €24 per child
• **Newport Bay Club** - €30 per adult, €24 per child

• **Hotel New York (The Art of Marvel)** - €32 per adult, €26 per child
• **Disneyland Hotel** - €45 per adult, €36 per child

To eat breakfast in the park at *Plaza Gardens* with Disney characters, the full price is €50 per adult and €40 per child - guests with a Meal Plan simply pay the difference. Breakfast is also available with the Princesses at L'*Auberge de Cendrillon* (€60 per adult, please check availability at the time of your visit).

Restaurant Types:

Buffet – All-you-can-eat locations where you fill your plate from the food selection as often as you want. Buffets only include one drink as it is illegal to offer unlimited soft drinks in France. Additional drinks will be charged at the end of your meal.

Quick Service – Fast food. Check out the menu, pay and collect the food a few minutes later. You will find everything from burgers and chips, to chicken, pizza and pasta. Disney's 'fast'-food locations are notoriously slow, and a queue of just four or five people in front of you can easily be a wait time of 20 to 30 minutes. If *Mobile Order* is an option, use this in-app service to save time.

Table Service – Order from a menu. A waiter brings the food to your table.

Character Dining – Characters interact with you and pose for photos as you dine.

Top Tip: You are not obliged to order from a set menu at most locations. Ordering specific items 'a la carte' is completely fine - although it may save you money if you order certain set menu combinations.

Disneyland Park

Disneyland Park is the main theme park at Disneyland Paris. It is made up of five lands filled with fantasy, adventure and excitement.

Disneyland Park, also known as *Parc Disneyland* in French, is based on the original Disneyland theme park that opened in California in 1955. Every Disney resort around the world has one of these classic "*Magic Kingdom*-style" Disney parks. The park spans 140 acres, almost twice the original's size.

Disneyland Park is Europe's most visited theme park and the ninth most visited in the world, with over 10 million yearly visitors. The park has plenty to offer guests, with almost fifty attractions (rides, themed areas and shows), character experiences, dining options and plenty of places to shop.

Disneyland Park is often called the most beautiful Disney theme park in the world.

The park is divided into five areas (or "lands") around *Sleeping Beauty Castle* in the centre. These are *Main Street USA, Frontierland, Adventureland, Fantasyland* and *Discoveryland*. Each land has its own overarching theme, with a unique soundtrack, décor, costumes and themed attractions. Around the edge of the park, you will find the *Disneyland Railroad*, which transports guests between these different lands.

As queuing is inevitable at theme parks, to help you prepare for how long you may wait to experience the attractions, we have included "average wait times"; these are for peak times such as school holidays (Summer, Christmas, Easter, half term) and weekends throughout the year. Wait times outside busy times are often lower.

☆	Is Disney Premier Access available? (see page 28)	⇕	Minimum height (in metres)
📷	Is there an On-Ride Photo?	🕐	Attraction Length
⧖	Average wait times (on peak days)		

Main Street, U.S.A.

Main Street, U.S.A. is the entrance to Disneyland Park, taking you to Sleeping Beauty Castle and beyond.

Main Street, U.S.A. is the entrance area of *Disneyland Park*, leading you towards *Sleeping Beauty Castle*. It is themed to look like 1920s America.

Main Street, U.S.A. has several shops on both sides of the street, the king of which is the **Emporium** where you are sure to find something to buy!

There are places to eat up and down the street, including Quick Service and Table Service restaurants, as well as snack locations. There are also other food shops and carts around *Main Street, U.S.A.*

Before entering *Main Street, U.S.A.*, you will see *Town Square* with a gazebo in the centre.

City Hall is immediately to the left on *Town Square*; this is "Guest Services". Here you can ask any questions you have, make reservations for VIP tours and restaurants, make complaints and leave positive feedback.

For disabled guests, an accessibility card is available at *City Hall*, providing easier access to attractions. See our 'Guests with Disabilities' chapter on page 81 for more information.

Running parallel to *Main Street, U.S.A.,* are the **Liberty Arcade** and **Discovery Arcade**. These provide an alternative covered route through the park, which is especially useful when it is raining or when the parade or fireworks are on. The Disney *Imagineers* learnt a valuable lesson from the other Disney theme parks, where *Main Street, U.S.A.* often became congested throughout the day.

You will often find character meet and greets in this area of the park, as well as live music.

Top Tip: As you walk up *Main Street, U.S.A.*, listen to the sounds from the windows on the first floor to hear the noise the town's residents make. You can hear a dentist in one window, a man taking a bath in another and even a piano recital!

Dining Key:
€ (Under €16)
€€ (€16 to €29)
€€€ (€30 to €39)
€€€€ (€40 to €49)
€€€€€ (€50+)

Prices relate to set menus for one person where available.

The in-park restaurants accept all Meal Plans, except *Auberge de Cendrillon,* which only takes the Premium Meal Plan. Learn more about Meal Plans on page 39.

[M] means Mobile Order is available (see page 36 for more info)

Main Street Vehicles and Horse-Drawn Street Cars

What better way to see *Main Street, U.S.A.* than from a vehicle – whether it is a horse-drawn car, a double-decker bus or one of the other modes of transport.

These vehicles typically only operate in the morning. You simply wait for the next vehicle to turn up at designated spots on *Town Square* and on *Central Plaza* in front of the park's iconic castle - look out for the lampposts with a sign saying 'City Vehicle Stop.'

Throughout the day, at unannounced times, the fountains in the moat around Sleeping Beauty Castle come to life with music, for special 2 to 3-minute shows. This takes place eight times per day but no schedule is officially published. If you are there on the hour or at half past the hour, you are more likely to see these.

These short fountain shows have seasonal variations during Halloween and Christmas, for example. They're a great extra surprise.

Disneyland Railroad - Main Street, U.S.A. Station

Take a grand tour of *Disneyland Park* onboard an authentic steam train. Whether you use it as a form of transportation or just a way of seeing the sights, the *Disneyland Railroad* is a fun way to enjoy the park. You even get to peek inside *Pirates of the Caribbean* along the route.

A full trip around the park takes about 20 minutes.

This attraction usually stops operating several hours before the park closes (and also temporarily during the daily parade).

Dining
Walt's Restaurant (€€€€€) – Table Service with French and international food. Each room is themed to a different land of *Parc Disneyland*.
Casey's Corner [M] (€) – Counter Service. Serves ballgame-themed snacks such as classic hot dogs and chicken nuggets. Also serves, salads, desserts and hot and cold drinks.
Plaza Gardens Restaurant (€€€€ to €€€€€) – Buffet. The character breakfast is €50 per adult and €40 per child. A lunch buffet (no characters) costs €45 per adult and €25 per child. A dinner buffet with Disney characters is €80 per adult and €40 per child.
Victoria's Home-Style Restaurant (€) – Counter Service. Hot and cold drinks are €3 to €5. Serves milkshakes in warmer months. Serves Mickey Waffles seasonally.
Market House Deli (€) – Counter Service and Snacks. Serves sandwiches and coffees.
Cookie Kitchen and Cable Car Bake Shop (€) – Counter Service for *Cable Car Bake Shop* and take-away for *Cookie Kitchen*. Serves cookies, muffins and pastries as well as drinks.
The Gibson Girl Ice Cream Parlour (€) – Take-away only ice cream location. May also serve Mickey Waffles during colder months. Ice creams cost around €5.

Frontierland

Step into Frontierland and be transported to the Wild Western town of Thunder Mesa.

As well as the attractions featured on the following pages, you may also wish to visit **Rustler Roundup Shootin' Gallery**, where you can practice your shooting skills in a carnival-style game. There is an additional charge for this attraction. Other attractions in this land include the **Disneyland Railroad's Frontierland Station**, and **Pocahontas Indian Village** - a themed outdoor playground.

Big Thunder Mountain

According to Disney legend, Big Thunder Mountain and the town of Thunder Mesa were discovered in the late 1800s.

In the town, a train line was constructed to transport ore around the mountain. However, the town was cursed, and it was soon struck by an earthquake.

Residents left the town, but a few years later, the trains were found driving themselves around the mountain.

Guests can now take a 4-minute ride in one of these mine trains for themselves.

Along the way, you will see collapsing bridges, experience a dynamite blast, dive under bats and much more on this wild ride!

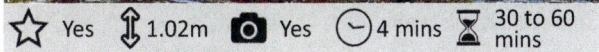

☆ Yes ⇕ 1.02m 📷 Yes 🕐 4 mins ⏳ 30 to 60 mins

Most of the action takes place on an island in the middle of the lake, making it a unique version of the ride compared to other Disney theme parks around the world.

It is also the longest, tallest and fastest *Big Thunder Mountain*, but it is easily the most kid-friendly of

Disneyland Paris' roller coasters.

At the end, you can buy your on-ride photo if you wish.

This is one of our favourite attractions in the park and should not be missed by those who enjoy a thrill.

Lion King: Rhythms of the Pride Lands

See this theatre-style production of *The Lion King*. In this 30-minute show, you'll be dazzled by acrobats, dancers and live singers.

Entry into the show is included in your park admission. We recommend arriving at least 45 minutes early (check the app for showtimes) as seats are

limited.

Alternatively, you can pay €15 in the Disneyland Paris app to book a seat in advance and guarantee entry - even with this, we'd still recommend turning up 30 minutes before showtime for the best view. We don't recommend paying for this service.

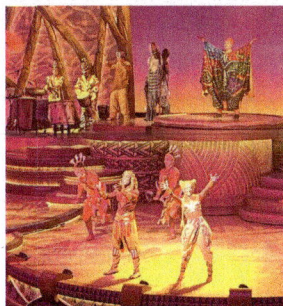

Phantom Manor

☆ Yes   ↕ None   📷 No   🕐 7 mins   ⧖ Less than 30 mins

Phantom Manor is a must-see attraction: the atmosphere, music, and details are among the best at Disneyland Paris.

Phantom Manor is a themed ride. It is not a horror-maze attraction with actors jumping out to scare you, and as there is no minimum height restriction, the attraction is accessible to all ages. However, do be wary of frightening younger kids.

After a walk-through section in the manor's lobby and other rooms introducing the story, you'll sit in "doombuggies" for the ride portion of the attraction. These rotate and tilt to show you the manor as they travel along the ride path.

You can expect to see pianos and door knockers with a mind of their own, a seance, and ghosts gathering for a ballroom dance.

Throughout the attraction, there are no jump-out scares, but the initial walk-through section may frighten some children due to the effects used here, and the dark. The animatronics in the cemetery scene may also frighten young children. These all pass by relatively quickly, and for every slightly scary moment, there is a fun moment or two.

If you are unsure whether your child will be comfortable with the ride, try doing it during the daytime when the building's exterior looks less imposing. You could also try watching an on-ride video online before visiting to see if it is suitable.

If you are unsure of whether your kids will enjoy it, we recommend *not* making this your first ride as riding this at the start of a trip can make kids apprehensive about all other rides - even if they are very different.

We highly recommend making a stop at this ride as it is a true Disney classic, and as the ride's main character, Melanie says: "Be sure to bring your death certificate. We're just dying to have you."

Phantom Manor has a dark storyline: on her wedding day, Melanie Ravenswood eagerly awaited her groom, not knowing that a phantom haunted the house she was in. The phantom (Melanie's father) lured the groom into the attic and hanged him. Melanie waited for her groom, but he never turned up. Now, she roams around the manor still in her wedding dress. Today, you venture through this derelict manor as you discover Melanie's story.

The storyline of this attraction is unique, despite similar *Haunted Mansion*-style rides existing at other Disney parks worldwide.

Thunder Mesa Riverboat Landing

Set sail on a classic riverboat around *Big Thunder Mountain* and admire *Frontierland's* scenery. The riverboat is a relaxing change of pace from the crowds in the park and there is plenty of space to roam around the boat.

There is some limited

☆ No   ⬍ None   ⏱ 15 minutes   ⏳ Less than 30 minutes

seating and you can listen to the story of the Molly Brown riverboat on the speakers as you sail along the river. Most people just take in the atmosphere, as the audio is not particularly loud.

Top Tip: The *Riverboat's* operating hours are shorter than many other attractions. It typically closes in the middle of the afternoon or early evening.

There's More to Frontierland Than Meets The Eye

As well as the major attractions featured here, you should enjoy the little details that make *Frontierland* unique. As you walk into *Frontierland* from *Central Plaza*, stop by **Fort Comstock**, the timber-themed entrance to the land. Notice the little details here, and if the steps are open on the left, climb up for a different perspective on this part of the park.

Phantom Manor has its own cemetery at the exit called **Boot Hill**. This area contains tombstones of several Thunder Mesa residents, all telling their own stories through gags and rhymes (in English). When you leave the attraction, you can turn right down the hill to the front of the manor or continue straight ahead to Boot Hill. You can also access Boot Hill without riding *Phantom Manor* by walking up the hill to the right of the manor.

Even the restaurants and shops are filled with details. **The Lucky Nugget Saloon** hosts live music and other acts. **Cowboy Cookout BBQ** also has live music, and Disney's engineers *(Imagineers)* went to town with the theming. Notice the chairs, for example - unlike other restaurants where everything is uniform, here there are many different types and styles of chairs because, in the Wild West, the townsfolk would bring chairs from home.

Dining

Silver Spur Steakhouse (€€€ to €€€€) – Table Service. Steakhouse and grill.
The Lucky Nugget Saloon (€€) – Counter/Table Service-hybrid serving American fare.
Cowboy Cookout Barbecue [M] (€€) – Counter Service serving Tex-Mex & BBQ food.
Casa de Coco [M] (€ to €€) – Counter Service serving Tex-Mex fare, mainly burritos.
Last Chance Cafe [M] (€) – Counter Service. Take-away snacks such as chicken drumsticks, vegan chilli 'con carne', salads and snakcs. Also sells desserts, beer, hot and cold drinks.

Adventureland

Venture into an Arabian story, the Caribbean or a temple with Indiana Jones.

In addition to the attractions covered below, you may also want to check out **Adventure Isle** (a walkthrough area with winding paths, caves, a pirate ship, and a suspension bridge), **Le Passage Enchanté d'Aladdin** (a walkthrough attraction with scenes from the story of *Aladdin*) and **La Plage des Pirates** (an outdoor playground).

Indiana Jones et le Temple du Péril

This rollercoaster will take you on an archaeological adventure through the lost Temple of Doom.

Your adventure will have you climbing in search of treasure, dropping and turning around tight corners, and meandering in and around the temple. You will even descend rapidly into a 360-degree loop as your mine cart goes 'out of control'.

☆ Yes   ↕ 1.40m   📷 No   ⏱ 2 mins   ⏳ 25 to 45 mins

The ride has the biggest minimum height limit of any ride at any Disney park worldwide – 140cm (about 55"). It was also the first Disney rollercoaster in the world to go upside down. The ride even ran backwards for a few years but now runs forward again.

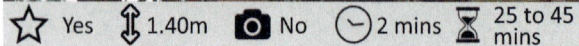

This is one of the resort's most intense coasters, with the loop being particularly tight. It is also quite a rough ride.

Of all the coasters in the park, this one usually has the shortest queue as it is hidden at the back of the park, and the minimum height limit means it is off-limits to most kids under the age of 10. Overall, it is a relatively short but fun experience.

Top Tip 1: Although this attraction sometimes gets long wait times, it is often much less busy after the daily parade.

Top Tip 2: This attraction offers a *Single Rider* queue.

Disneyland Park

Pirates of the Caribbean

Ahoy, me hearties! Set sail through the world of *Pirates of the Caribbean* at Disneyland Paris.

Board a boat and enjoy a journey into a fort invaded by pirates. You'll float by scenes with amazing audio-animatronic characters bringing the action to life. Your boat will go down two short drops, so be warned - *ye may get wet!*

☆ Yes   ↕ None   📷 Yes   🕐 10 mins   ⧖ 15 to 45 mins

It may just be the best-themed attraction in all of *Disneyland Park*. The attention to detail is fantastic, from the queue line to the *Cast Members'* costumes and the music to the sets.

This attraction is based on the original *Pirates of the Caribbean* ride at Disneyland in California. *Pirates of the Caribbean* was the final ride Walt Disney himself supervised the creation of at Disneyland.

The ride now also includes well-known film characters like Jack Sparrow, Blackbeard and Barbossa.

Be aware that the queue line for the ride is not well-lit due to the atmosphere it aims to create, and is very dark. This will especially strike you when riding during the daytime as your eyes take a while to adjust, so watch your step and hold onto your children's hands in the queue line.

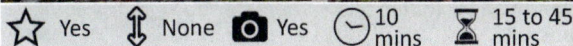

Each boat can take 23 passengers, so the queue is always moving, but it is also a popular ride. This means that most of the year wait times stay below 20 minutes, but these rise to 60 minutes on peak days. As you wait, there is a lot to see in the indoor section - the attention to detail is amazing. If the wait is over 30 minutes, we recommend you come back later as it will subside.

The *recommended* minimum age for this attraction is 12 months old as it is dark and loud, however, no age limit is officially imposed.

This is a must-see, family-friendly ride that is a classic Disney experience.

Warning: As the queue line for this attraction is so dark and there are so many people in one place, sadly, it is a favourite spot for pickpockets – especially when there are long waits. Be aware of your surroundings and keep an eye on your belongings - even at Disneyland Paris.

The Independent Guide to Disneyland Paris 2025   49

La Cabane des Robinson

Enter the world of Swiss Family Robinson as you explore the treehouse made from the wood of their shipwreck. You can see the complex water wheel system they built to get water up to the bedrooms, and explore the kitchen, living rooms and bedrooms.

This is a walkthrough experience and kids love exploring and climbing the steps.

☆ No   ↕ None   📷 No   🕐 5 mins   ⧗ None

The view is mostly obscured from the top by the tree's leaves, but you can get an interesting perspective on the park from up here.

Adventureland is designed to be explored on foot...

Of all the lands at *Disneyland Park*, *Adventureland* is the one that appears to have the smallest number of attractions. However, this area of the park is filled with incredible details that you need to find for yourself outside of the main attractions.

Adventureland is built around *Adventure Isle*, with *La Cabane des Robinson* at the centre. As well as the treehouse, be sure to step aboard the **Pirate Galleon** moored in the centre of the land, and explore the caves under the treehouse to see the secrets that lie here. There is also another set of **caves** next to the galleon - here, you will find treasure, skeletons and cascading waterfalls.

Follow the signs to **"Pont Suspendu"** to reach Spyglass Hill and enjoy the stunning view over the park. Don't forget to cross the wobbly Suspension Bridge and the Floating Bridge (**"Pont Flotant"**) right next to the Swiss Family Robinson's shipwreck.

Dining

Agrabah Cafe (€€€€) – Buffet specialising in North African cuisine themed to a bazaar.
Captain Jack's (€€€€) – Table Service with international food options. This restaurant is inside the *Pirates of the Caribbean* ride building, so you can see the boats sail by as you eat.
Colonel Hathi's Pizza Outpost (€ to €€) – Counter Service with Italian and Indian options such as pasta, pizza and butter chicken.
Cool Post (€) – Snacks such as popcorn and ice creams. Plus, hot and cold drinks.
Restaurant Hakuna Matata [M] (€€) – Counter Service with a constantly changing menu; it usually offers more creative choices than just burgers, pizzas and fries.

Fantasyland

Find classic Disney attractions in this land dedicated to the young and the young at heart.

Disneyland Park's gentle toddler-friendly rides are found here in the most magical of all the lands, and *Fantasyland* has *plenty* of variety. In addition to the attractions covered on the following pages, you may also want to visit **The Dragon's Lair** *(La Tanière du Dragon)* and **Sleeping Beauty's Gallery** *(La Galerie de la Belle au Bois Dormant).* These are both great detailed walk-through attractions inside the park's castle. *The Dragon's Lair* contains a huge animatronic dragon (more on page 54).

Important Note: *Fantasyland* closes one hour before the rest of the park each day to clear the area for the nightly fireworks show.

Peter Pan's Flight

Hop aboard a flying pirate ship and voyage through the world of Peter Pan and Neverland.

As you soar, you will see scenes to the sides and underneath you in a retelling of the classic story.

Peter Pan's Flight is one of Disneyland Paris' most popular rides. It features beloved characters, is family-friendly and provides a small thrill too.

The ride's interior is stunning from the moment you step inside and is truly immersive.

This is an incredibly popular ride - to minimise wait times, visit it early in the

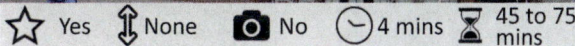

☆ Yes	⇕ None	📷 No	🕐 4 mins	⏳ 45 to 75 mins

morning, in the evening just before *Fantasyland* closes, or during the parade.

Important: Visitors afraid of heights may want to skip this ride. The ships you sit in make it feel like you are really flying, and at times

you will be several metres off the ground and descending steeply (but not quickly). This may surprise some guests. Mostly, though, it seems to be adults who are affected by this, and not children.

Lancelot's Carousel

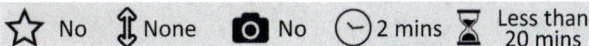

☆ No	⇕ None	📷 No	🕐 2 mins	⏳ Less than 20 mins

This is a beautiful vintage carousel right in the middle of *Fantasyland*. It is lined with golden horses and is a joy to ride for people of all ages.

Waits for this ride are fairly consistent throughout the

day but get shorter later in the day and during the daily parade.

Although you can find carousels in almost any theme park, something about this one feels extra magical.

Alice's Curious Labyrinth

Have you ever fancied getting lost in the world of *Alice in Wonderland*? Well, now is your chance!

This maze is just challenging enough to keep you guessing where to go next. There are photo opportunities around every corner (or should we say hedge) along the way.

Once you reach the end of the maze, you can return to the park or climb the Queen of Hearts' castle first. The climb is worth doing for the stunning view over the park.

| ☆ No | ↕ None | 📷 No | ◷ 10 mins | ⧗ None |

The labyrinth is great family fun and a good way for the little ones to burn some energy.

Meet Mickey Mouse

Mickey is preparing backstage for his next magic show, and you have the chance to meet him. While queuing in the indoor area, you can watch short films playing on a big screen.

Once you reach the front, you will enter a room with Mickey. Here you can meet the big cheese himself, chat, and get an autograph and photos.

| ☆ No | ↕ None | 📷 Yes | ◷ 1 to 2 mins | ⧗ 45 to 75 minutes |

You are welcome to take your own photos or ask the *Cast Member* here to help you. Plus, a Disney photographer will also take an 'official' photo, which you can buy at the attraction's exit.

Princess Pavilion

| ☆ No | ↕ None | 📷 Yes | ◷ 2 minutes | ⧗ 45 to 90 minutes |

Princess Pavilion is your chance to meet one of the Disney princesses. Then chat, get an autograph and take some photos.

Outside the attraction, a sign tells you which princesses you will meet at the end of the queue and the time each princess is available for meet and greets.

If seeing a particular princess is a priority, we suggest you visit *Princess Pavilion* as early as possible, as queue lines build up quickly.

Note that queues for this attraction can be long from the start of the day as it typically operates during *Extra Magic Time*.

Top Tip: A free activity booklet to keep you entertained may be available - ask a Cast Member.

"it's a small world"

"it's a small world" is one of the resort's most memorable and popular attractions, featuring hundreds of dolls singing a catchy song about the uniting of the world.

Guests travel leisurely on boats through scenes representing countries from around the world.

With boats taking lots of passengers, queues are often short. If the wait is more than 20 minutes, come back later in the day.

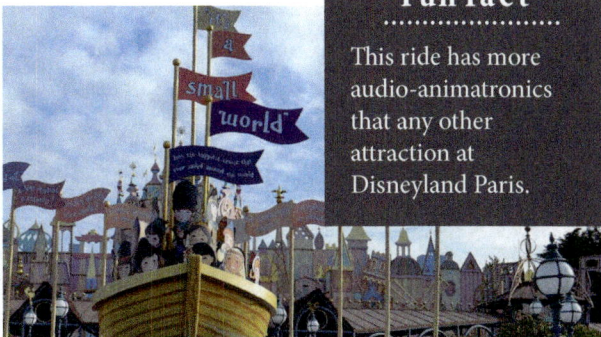

Fun Fact

This ride has more audio-animatronics that any other attraction at Disneyland Paris.

☆ Yes ↕ None 📷 No 🕐 10 mins ⧗ Less than 20 mins

This ride is a great Disney classic and is one of the "must-dos" for many visitors.

Blanche Neige et les Sept Nains

☆ No ↕ None 📷 No 🕐 2 mins ⧗ 20 to 40 minutes

Relive the tale of *Snow White* for yourself in this classic ride filled with light-hearted scenes, and some darker moments too.

Although the ride itself is slow-moving, some moments may scare young children.

The Evil Witch, in particular, makes surprise appearances out of every corner, the dark woods have ominous trees, and thunder and lightning effects may startle younger children.

Mad Hatter's Teacups

⧗ Less than 20 minutes ☆ No 🕐 2 minutes ↕ None

Hop inside the Mad Hatter's teacup sand go for a wild spin. This is a theme park classic and great fun for all ages. You can control the spinning by turning the wheel in the centre.

The Adventures of Pinocchio

Ride through a retelling of the story of *Pinocchio* and see the tales from the book and film come to life.

As with the original story, some darker moments may frighten younger children, though these pass by quickly. It is much less frightening than the *Snow White* attraction above, for example.

This ride is not a major attraction like *Peter Pan's Flight*, but still draws in moderately sized queues

☆ No ↕ None 📷 No 🕐 2 mins ⧗ 20 to 45 minutes

due to the popular characters.

Sleeping Beauty Castle - Le Château de la Belle au Bois Dormant

Standing 51m (167ft) tall, *Le Château de la Belle au Bois Dormant*, is the centrepiece and icon of *Disneyland Park*.

When the *Imagineers* were designing *Disneyland Park*, they knew that the castle here had to be unique and very different from the castles in the American Disney theme parks. Europeans were used to seeing real castles, so the park's icon had to be more fairytale-inspired than real.

The attention to detail is stunning, even including little snails (or *escargots*) on the turrets at the top, and the trees in front of the castle are pruned into a square shape, just like in the 1959 *Sleeping Beauty* film.

The castle is not just for show; you can explore it. On the ground floor, you can walk along the drawbridge and over the moat to enjoy this magical building from the inside.

To the right-hand side of the castle, you can see a small wishing well where Disney characters occasionally meet guests - it's a great photo spot.

Behind the castle, you can find the **Sword in the Stone**. Try to pull it out and you could be crowned king or queen of the kingdom.

Inside the castle, you can enjoy two unique shops, which are incredibly well-themed: Merlin the Magician's shop on the left and a year-round Christmas shop *(La Boutique du Château)* on the right.

Once you have finished shopping, take the winding staircase up to the first floor and see the story of Sleeping Beauty retold using **tapestries** and beautiful stained-glass windows in *La Galerie de la Belle au Bois Dormant*. You can even step onto the balcony outside for a stunning view over *Fantasyland*.

The castle's biggest secret, however, is hidden. Looking at the castle from the front, take the path on the left instead of the drawbridge. This leads you through a dark passageway and underground into **The Dragon's Lair** *(La Tanière du Dragon)*. You can also access the dragon's lair through Merlin's shop.

Here you'll find an enormous animatronic dragon (at the time, the biggest ever built) set in a unique area that's unlike anything found at other Disney theme parks worldwide. The dragon comes to life every few minutes - but don't worry, it doesn't breathe fire!

Dumbo - The Flying Elephant

☆ No   ↕ None   📷 No   🕐 90 seconds   ⏳ 45 to 75 minutes

Dumbo is one of the most popular rides at Disneyland Paris.

Located right in the centre of *Fantasyland*, it offers views of the surrounding area and is a lot of fun.

In each flying elephant,

there is a lever that allows you to lift your Dumbo up or down and fly up to 7 metres (23ft) high!

As the ride is popular and has a low capacity, there are long waits all day. Ride it during the parade, during *Extra Magic Time*, or at the

start or end of the day for the shortest waits.

The colourful scenery and whimsical music will transport you to a world of pure imagination. This ride is perfect for families with young children or anyone looking for a nostalgic ride.

Casey Jr: The Circus Train

Based on the character from *Dumbo*, *Casey Junior* is the little circus train that will take you on a ride around models of sets from classic Disney films.

This is a great ride for the whole family. Although it is not a rollercoaster, it can be a good way of seeing whether the kids (or adults) are up to a slightly wilder ride - though this ride is still very tame compared to the other more thrilling rides at the parks.

Adults may feel cramped on this ride with minimal leg and headroom. There is no height restriction, so everyone can ride, and the low speed is unlikely to frighten anyone.

☆ No   ↕ None   📷 No   🕐 2 mins   ⏳ 20 to 40 minutes

During your ride, you will whizz by castles and other story pieces from Disney's classic tales. Try the *Storybook Canal Boats* right next door for a more leisurely view of these scenes.

Unfortunately, the ride is often only open for limited periods during the off-season. It also often closes 2 to 3 hours before the rest of *Fantasyland*, so look out for a sign near the attraction entrance showing its opening hours.

Le Pays des Contes de Fees - Storybook Canal Boats

This is a nice, relaxing ride, where you sail by models of classic childhood tales on a boat.

Along your serene journey, you will see scenes from *The Little Mermaid, Hansel and Gretel, Fantasia, Snow White, Frozen, Winnie the Pooh, Up* and many more films.

You will even enter the famous cave from *Aladdin*, and see Genie's lamp shining brightly.

It is a nice change of pace from some of the busier attractions in the park, and you can take some great photos of the models.

This is a great attraction for very young children who can

☆ No   ↕ None   📷 No   🕐 5 mins   ⧗ Less than 20 mins

look around without anything potentially being scary.

If you want a different perspective on these scenes at a faster pace, consider riding *Casey Junior* instead.

This attraction almost

always has low wait times, and many people do not know this part of the park exists.

This attraction often closes two to three hours before the rest of *Fantasyland* and may be closed during the off-season.

Dining

Auberge de Cendrillon (€€€€€) – Table Service. At this restaurant, the Disney Princesses (and their accompanying princes) roam. They will dance throughout the meal, and visit every table to meet guests too for chats and photos. This meal can be pre-booked and pre-paid as part of a Disneyland Paris package. Breakfast with the Disney Princesses is also available. The only Meal Plan accepted here is the Premium Meal Plan. The adult set menu is €100 (€120 with wine) and the child set menu is €50.

Au Chalet de la Marionette [M] (€ to €€) – Counter Service with an international menu.

Pizzeria Bella Notte (€ to €€) – Counter Service. Serves pizza and pasta.

Toad Hall Restaurant (€) – Counter Service. Serves British fare such as fish and chips, and international food such as chicken sandwiches.

The Old Mill (€) – Snack location. Serves crisps, cakes, ice creams, and hot & cold drinks.

Discoveryland

Take a look into the future… from the minds of the past. Discoveryland is inspired by retro-futuristic visions of space and beyond.

Some of the park's most popular and thrilling attractions are located in this land. In addition to the attractions listed below, you can hop on a train for a trip around the park from **Disneyland Railroad's Discoveryland Station**.

Star Wars Hyperspace Mountain: Rebel Mission

Hyperspace Mountain is a thrilling rollercoaster through space and our favourite coaster at the resort.

Space Mountain is a common fixture at Disney parks around the world but this is the only *Space Mountain* to flip you upside down, as well as a high-speed launch. It is also the grandest and most extreme of all the *Space Mountain* rides around the world. The beautiful steampunk-style building is the centrepiece of *Discoveryland*.

At the moment, this ride has a *Star Wars* overlay. As you soar through the galaxy, you'll encounter TIE fighters, Star Destroyers, and other

☆ Yes ⇕ 1.20m ◔ 2 mins 📷 Yes ⧗ 45 to 75 minutes

iconic *Star Wars* spacecraft. The special effects and sounds of blasters and explosions make you feel like you're in an epic space battle. It's a must-do ride for thrill-seekers!

Top Tip: This ride has a *Single Rider* queue line, so if you are alone, or do not mind being separated from your party, you can use it to drastically reduce your wait time.

Mickey's PhilharMagic - Discoveryland Theatre

Philharmagic is a fun 4D theatre show for the whole family.

The story is that you are attending Goofy's opera performance with Mickey's Philharmonic orchestra. When Donald gets involved, however, things get a little out of hand, and you end up on an adventure travelling through a world of Disney classic movies.

With an air-conditioned theatre, shelter from the rain and a fantastic musical movie, it is easy to see why this attraction is one of our favourites.

Waits are usually non-existent as shows run back-to-back throughout the day.

Expect scenes and songs from *The Little Mermaid*, *Coco*, *Aladdin* and more.

Les Mystères du Nautilus

Explore Captain Nemo's ship, the Nautilus, from the Jules Nerve novel *20,000 Leagues Under the Sea*.

This incredibly detailed walkthrough attraction takes you under the sea and into the heart of the submarine.

Les Mystères du Nautilus is a work of art and includes special effects such as a giant squid attack, as well as an incredible level of theming and detail. You'll see detailed replicas of the Nautilus' features, including the famous organ played by Captain Nemo.

It also features narration in both French and English, providing insights into the story and history of the *Nautilus*.

☆ No   ↕ None   📷 No   🕐 5 mins   ⧗ None

In general, young kids are unlikely to be entertained as it is a simple walkthrough with little interactivity.

Insider Secret: Although you may believe you are inside the *Nautilus* ship in the lagoon, the winding staircase you use to enter this attraction is designed to disorientate you. You actually walk down a long corridor and into a show building between *Autopia* and *Discoveryland Theatre* – the exact opposite direction from the *Nautilus*.

Autopia

☆ Yes   ↕ See notes   📷 No   🕐 5 minutes   ⧗ 30 to 60 minutes

Hop aboard one of these little cars and take it for a spin around *Discoveryland*. *Autopia* is hugely popular with kids who get to drive a car for the very first time.

The cars are guided on rails,

so you can't go too far wrong, but the little ones (and bigger ones also) can steer and accelerate around the track and 'race' others.

The ride is fun, but wait times are often long.

Height information: Riders under 0.81m may not ride. Riders between 0.81m and 1.32m must be accompanied by someone over the 1.32m height minimum. Riders over 1.32m may ride alone.

Orbitron: Machines Volantes

☆ Yes   ↕ None   📷 No   🕐 90 seconds   ⧗ 30 to 60 minutes

Soar above *Discoveryland* in your very own spaceship.

This is a spinning-type ride similar to *Dumbo* in *Fantasyland*, but the ships

here go higher, spin faster and tilt more, making for a surprisingly good thrill.

It is a lot of fun, but it is not a must-do attraction.

Note: It is a very tight fit for two adults in one spaceship, so avoid this. An adult and a child should fit in a spaceship fine, however.

> A *Star Wars* character meet and greet location called "StarPort" is available in front of *Star Tours* featuring Darth Vader, and occasionally other characters such as Kylo Ren.

Star Tours: The Adventures Continue

Star Tours is a 3D simulator-style attraction based on *Star Wars.*

In the queue line, you enter an intergalactic spaceport. As you travel through the terminal, you will see Star-Speeders (your transport vehicle), an alien air traffic control station, R2-D2, C3PO, and many robots hard at work to make your journey to space unforgettable.

☆ Yes ⬍ 1.02m 🕐 5 mins 📷 No ⏳ 30 to 45 mins

You will then board your StarSpeeder for a trip to one of many planets from the *Star Wars* universe.

With over 50 randomised scenes, you never know what planet you will explore on your ride.

Most of the dialogue is in French, but it is the visuals

and the movement that matter here; the simulator feels incredibly realistic! This is a definite must-do. This attraction is equally fun for those who have never seen the films.

Be advised that if you are

prone to motion sickness, or dislike confined spaces, you should skip *Star Tours.*

Top Tip: If you want a milder ride, ask to be seated in the front row. This is the centre of the ride vehicle and reduces the movement you will feel. For a more thrilling experience, ask for the back row.

Buzz Lightyear Laser Blast

Join Buzz Lightyear on a mission to defeat the evil Emperor Zurg and save the universe.

Once on the ride, guests board a space cruiser and use laser blasters to shoot targets, earning points for each hit. There are even hidden targets which score you thousands of bonus points.

At the end of the ride, the person with the most points wins. It is competitive, fun and re-rideable – it is also a great family adventure with no minimum height limit.

☆ Yes ⬍ None 📷 Yes 🕐 5 mins ⏳ 45 to 75 mins

If you buy an on-ride photo at the end, you can get your score printed on it too!

Top Tip: The highest-scoring target is directly in front of Zurg – shoot his medallion repeatedly for extra points.

Dining

Cafe Hyperion [M] (€ to €€) – Counter Service serving American-style fast-food (mainly burgers). There are digital menu terminals you can use but Mobile Order is still faster.

Fireworks

Disney theme parks around the world are renowned for ending visitors' days by lighting up the sky with incredible firework displays. Disneyland Paris is no exception.

Top Tips

1: For the best *Disney Tales of Magic* spot, we recommend you arrive at least 60 minutes before the show begins. Some guests get spots even earlier than this. You will find people staking out the best spots 2 hours before the show begins.

2: Find a spot with a railing in front of you – this prevents someone from turning up during the show and blocking your view. This often happens when guests put their children on their shoulders, ruining the view for everyone behind.

3: After the show, only *Main Street, U.S.A.* remains open. There are three main toilet locations for you to use – the first, and the least crowded, is located by the Baby Care Center (Zone J on the map overleaf). The second is inside the arcades running alongside *Main Street*. The third is at the end of *Main Street, U.S.A.* and to the right of the *Disneyland Railroad* station at the Arboretum (Zone P).

4: If you want to save yourself the hassle of finding a spot consider buying a *Disney Premier Access* for the reserved viewing area at the front (approx €19-€22).

Disney Tales of Magic is Disneyland Paris' brand new dazzling nighttime spectacular featuring music, projections, lasers, drones, water fountains and fireworks.

The projections will also extend all the way along *Main Street U.S.A.* for the first time at Disneyland Paris instead of being limited to the castle.

This new show launches on 10th January 2025. Until then, the long-running *Disney Dreams* will be performed nightly instead.

You can expect scenes from *Lilo and Stitch, Encanto, Pinocchio, Beauty and the Beast, Frozen, Pocahontas, The Lion King, Peter Pan* and many more Disney and Pixar classics.

Disney Tales of Magic is performed nightly starting at the time of *Disneyland Park's* closing. The show runs for 20 minutes. After the show, *Main Street, U.S.A.,* remains open for about 45 minutes after the park closes for your shopping convenience.

Other fireworks shows are offered on select nights, such as Bastille Day and New Year's Eve. On these days, a themed firework display is performed first, followed by *Disney Tales of Magic*.

Walt Disney Studios Park features nighttime projection shows on the *Hollywood Tower Hotel* during particular seasons (more about seasonal events on pages 88-91).

Disney Tales of Magic Viewing Guide

Disney Tales of Magic is primarily a projection show so having a view of the front of *Sleeping Beauty Castle* is important.

Although the fireworks and drones can be seen from across the park, you will miss out on a lot if you are not viewing the front of the

castle and its projections.

The front is also where the lasers, fountains and fire effects can be seen.

You will want to position yourself at the park's *Central Plaza* (hub) area or along *Main Street, U.S.A.* for the best view.

To help you decide on the best view of *Disney Tales of Magic* we have created this helpful guide – note that we have invented the zones or areas in the diagram. There are no boundaries between the areas when you are in the park itself.

Zone A – A very off-centre view of the show. Not crowded, but this should be a last resort.

Zone B – A better view than from Zone A. Uncrowded but this is an off-centre view. Good if you want to see the show last minute from a decent angle. You may get wet here.

Zone C – This is the paid reserved viewing area for the nighttime show. You will see the projections clearly but may miss the grandeur of some of the drones. Personally, we think this zone is too close to *Sleeping Beauty Castle*. You may be lightly sprayed by the water fountains in this area.

Zone D – This area is often cleared by Cast Members and may or may not be open to guests. When the area *is* open, views are not ideal and very off-centre.

Zone E – Views from this area are obstructed by trees, with no visibility.

Zone F – Located off-centre. Behind and to the left of the nighttime show control booth. If you are positioned by the railing here, you will get a great (angled) view of the show – this location can only accommodate a few people.

Zone G – This is where guests who arrive early usually wait. This area provides a decent view of the show, and you will see all the fireworks and effects. It may, however, be too close to the action for you to appreciate the show fully, in our opinion. Part of this area may be reserved for people with disability cards and people accompanying them.

Zone H – Faces the castle head-on and is far back enough to provide a good view of the show. It is not a perfect view, but it is very good.

Zone I – Our favourite view of the show. It is the perfect distance from *Sleeping Beauty Castle*. If you stand by the railings surrounding the flowerbeds, you will have a near-perfect view of the show. Be aware of the large speakers and light poles getting in the way. You will not see the projections on *Main Street, U.S.A.* from here.

Zone J – A very off-centre view with many trees meaning poor visibility. This is improved in the winter when there is less foliage and some spots can be decent. When the trees have leaves in warmer months, this is not a good viewing location.

Zone K – Views are obstructed by trees and the *Disney Tales of Magic* control booth. No visibility.

Zone L – An excellent view; it is a good distance from the castle to see the full show effects while not feeling too distant. This area is also usually less crowded than Zone I. You are also closer to the park exit.

Zone M, N and O – These zones are located along *Main Street, U.S.A.* and provide an average view of the show. The closer you are to the castle here, the better. These zones are usually less crowded than zones closer to the castle. You will likely see many people with kids on their shoulders in front of you.

You do, however, get to see the projections on *Main Street, U.S.A.* all around you.

Zone P – No visibility.

Zone Q – Must be staked out very early and involves you standing on the bandstand in *Town Square* – there is very limited space here. Still, it provides an elevated view over other guests on *Main Street, U.S.A.* Specific projections are hard to see from here, but the unique view makes it worth considering. However, we would not recommend this view if you are seeing the show for the first time. At the end of the show, you are conveniently right by the park exit and well ahead of the crowds.

Parades

Disney Stars on Parade is the best way to see all your favourite Disney characters in one place as they parade through *Fantasyland*, around the castle hub and down *Main Street U.S.A.*

The parade is performed daily and the time varies day to day. Check the app for the exact schedule.

Characters in the parade may vary. Still, you can typically see about 50 characters and floats, including Tinker Bell, *Toy Story* characters, Simba, Nala, Baloo, Mowgli, Captain Hook, Peter Pan and characters from *Finding Dory*.

Other characters include Rapunzel, Cinderella, Snow White, Anna and Elsa.

It is not just the exciting characters - the floats are amazing too! One of these is a fire-breathing dragon that will take your breath away!

The most popular place to watch the parade is *Main Street, U.S.A.* You should secure your spot about one hour before the parade starts for the best view if watching from here. At other locations, 30-40 minutes should do.

The parade runs as normal during light or moderate rain. During heavy rain, or if there is a thunderstorm alert, the parade may be cancelled or delayed. In either case, an announcement is made at the parade start time.

During seasonal events smaller parades with three to five floats (dubbed *cavalcades*) may be performed several times a day in addition to the main parade.

A paid-for reserved viewing area is available at €19-22 per person if you don't want to stake a spot out too early.

Walt Disney Studios Park

Walt Disney Studios Park is the second, and newest, theme park at Disneyland Paris. Here you can go behind the scenes and experience the magic of the movies.

Walt Disney Studios Park opened in 2002 and has significantly expanded over the years. In general, the park targets teenagers and adults more than young children and contains several thrill rides. As this is a Disney Park, there are also, of course, several attractions for the younger family members.

Despite its expansion over the years, you would still be hard-pressed to spend an entire day in *Walt Disney Studios Park* due to its limited number of attractions. Disneyland Paris has stated that expanding the park and improving its offerings is a priority.

At the moment, Disney is significantly upgrading the park. It added an *Avengers* area recently, and a *World of Frozen* area with a new lake and grand avenue will arrive in 2026. The park will also be renamed *Disney Adventure World* soon.

With around 5.7 million visitors annually, *Walt Disney Studios Park* is Europe's third most popular theme park. However, it still only receives half the number of visitors its big brother, *Disneyland Park*, gets next door.

The park has six main areas: *Front Lot, Toon Studio, Production Courtyard, Toy Story Playland, Worlds of Pixar,* and *Avengers Campus.*

Dining Key:
€ (Under €16)
€€ (€16 to €29)
€€€ (€30 to €39)
€€€€ (€40 to €49)
€€€€€ (€50+)

Prices relate to set menus for one person where available.

All in-park restaurants accept Meal Plans. Learn more about these on page 39.

[M] Means Mobile Order is available (see page 36)

Front Lot

As you enter the park, you are in Front Lot. This contains the Fantasia fountain as well as a covered area with shops and restaurants.

Front Lot is the entrance area to *Walt Disney Studios Park*, and home to Disney *Studio 1* – an indoor shopping and dining area designed to resemble Hollywood at night. *Disney Studio 1* is the equivalent of *Main Street, U.S.A.* in *Disneyland Park*.

Sometimes there is street entertainment performed here.

Front Lot is home to *Studio Services* (Guest Services), where you can get assistance, make a complaint, leave positive feedback and apply for disability assistance cards. It is also home to *Shutterbugs*, the park's photography studio.

Front Lot is also commonly home to photo spots with Disney characters.

Note: As part of the grand transformation of this park, *Studio 1* is closed until Spring 2025. During this time, guests will take an outdoor route around the building and the restaurants and shops here will be closed. This area will soon be renamed *World Premiere*.

Dining - CLOSED UNTIL SPRING 2025
A new unannounced restaurant concept will open in Spring 2025 inside Studio 1- we expect this location to have Mobile Order capabilities.

Production Courtyard

Stitch Live!

☆ No	↕ None	📷 No	◔ 10 minutes	⧖ Until next show

In this interactive theatre show, you'll enter a special transmission room and, before you know it, a *Cast Member* will connect you and your fellow earthlings to Stitch and you will speak with him live from space.

Stitch is curious about how planet Earth works, so he will ask all sorts of strange questions to learn about our home.

This attraction is good fun. There are separate English and French shows.

The Twilight Zone: Tower of Terror

Feel what it is like to drop 124 feet (38m) as *The Twilight Zone: Tower of Terror* transports you to the fifth dimension.

Disney summarises: "One stormy night long ago, five people stepped through the door of an elevator and into a nightmare. That door is opening once again, and this time it's opening for you."

☆ Yes	↕ 1.02m	◔ 2 mins	📷 Yes	⧖ 30 to 60 minutes

Once you board a service elevator, you'll 'drop in'. The elevator is like a free-fall drop ride, except you are pulled down faster than gravity so you come out of your seat – luckily you have seatbelts! In a split second, the elevator changes from going up to down, creating a weightless feeling.

The atmosphere inside is immersive and is possibly the best theming at the parks. This is a fun and intense experience that WILL have you screaming.

The experience is different inside each elevator so be prepared for a surprise every time you ride.

This ride may close early if a fireworks show is scheduled at this park on the day of your visit.

TOGETHER: A Pixar Musical Adventure

This 30-minute stage show is a mix of on-stage and on-screen characters, sets, a live band & special effects.

At the start of the show, you'll meet Charlie, a kid who dreams of conducting the orchestra for a school end-of-year gala. But suddenly Charlie's precious music sheets are lost just before the concert! As Charlie falls asleep, Woody and his pals join forces to recover the sheets scattered throughout various Pixar stories.

A "Secure Your Seat" option is available for €15 per person if you don't want to wait and have a guaranteed prime seat.

Minnie's Musical Moment at Studio D

Join Minnie and her friend Jamie as they invite you to play the game "Name That Song". This show is primarily in French. T

This show lasts about 12 minutes.

This show will be performed until 30th March 2025.

Toon Studio and Worlds of Pixar

Top Tip

While waiting in the queue, connect to the local Wi-Fi network from any smartphone to play a unique Crush touchscreen game.

Crush's Coaster

Crush's Coaster is a unique attraction and the only of its kind in any Disney theme park worldwide.

Guests board turtle shells in groups of four, sitting back-to-back in pairs. The first few scenes are a slow-moving dark ride but then you reach the rollercoaster portion, where you spin as you ride the waves with Crush.

Although the ride may seem for young kids, don't be fooled - this is a wild, fast adventure, so read the warning signs outside first.

The popularity of the characters and the ride's low capacity means this ride regularly has one of the longest queues in the park.

☆ Yes	↕ 1.07m	📷 No	⌚ 2 mins	⏳ 60 to 90 mins

Even on less busy days, waits exceed 40 minutes, and it is common to see them over 90 minutes.

Ride *Crush's Coaster* first thing in the morning or just before the park closes for the shortest wait.

Top Tip: In the last hour before the park closes, a long wait time is often displayed to discourage people from getting in the queue.

Top Tip 2: The wait time for the *Single Rider* queue is often exaggerated.

Frozen: A Musical Invitation

☆ No	↕ None	📷 No	⌚ 30 minutes	⏳ Until Next Show

This attraction combines shows, meet and greets and other *Frozen*-themed experiences.

Guests move between three different rooms - the first is a log cabin with Anna and

Sven joined by Elsa.

Then, you'll move to Elsa's Ice Palace for a sing-along.

At the end, you will find Olaf, who you can meet and get photos with.

Paid guaranteed seating is available in the Disneyland Paris app for €15.

Note: This experience is on hiatus until 14th Feb 2025 inclusive.

Les Tapis Volants - Flying Carpets over Agrabah

☆ No	↕ None	📷 No	⌚ 90 seconds	⏳ Less than 30 minutes

Board one of Aladdin's flying carpets and fly over Agrabah.

The ride is a simple spinner

ride, similar to *Dumbo* and *Orbitron* (at *Disneyland Park*). This ride, however, often has shorter queues than those other rides.

You can raise and lower your carpet and tilt it backwards and forwards!

Ratatouille: The Adventure

Shrink down to the size of a rat and board your 'ratmobile' to travel through the streets of Paris, scurrying along rooftops and kitchens in this clever immersive ride.

Along your journey, special effects and giant screens put you in the heart of the action. Feel the heat from a grill, the chill of a refrigerator, and you may even get splashed once or twice. There are also different smells throughout.

Ratatouille vehicles do not follow a fixed track, taking slightly different paths for a unique experience each time.

☆ Yes ⇕ None 🕐 5 mins 📷 No ⏳ 30 to 60 minutes

This ride often has one of the longest waits in both theme parks. Sneakily, in the last hour of park operation, an inflated wait time is often displayed to discourage people from queuing.

A *Single Rider* line is available. This typically reduces wait times to less than 30 minutes and often to less than 15 minutes. On busy days, waits in this queue can reach 60 minutes.

Cars Road Trip

☆ Yes ⇕ None 📷 No 🕐 8 minutes ⏳ 15 to 30 minutes

Hop aboard a studio tram and see scenes from Disney Pixar's hit film *Cars*. This is a short but fun family adventure for all ages.

You'll see the biggest lugnut in the world, experience 'Cars-tastrophe Canyon', see Mater's junkyard creations including an Eiffel Tower made of car parts, and more.

Cars Quatre Roues Rallye

Hop in for a spin on Route 66 with the characters from Disney Pixar's *Cars*.

☆ No ⇕ None 🕐 90 secs 📷 No ⏳ 15 to 45 minutes

The ride is similar to the teacup ride in *Disneyland*

Park, but you spin faster and in different directions in this version.

Vehicles can accommodate up to 2 adults, plus 2 extra kids.

Animagique Theater – Mickey and the Magician

☆ No ⇕ None 📷 No 🕐 30 minutes ⏳ Shows at set times

Go back in time to Paris at the turn of the 19th century... enter a Magician's workshop, where the assistant is Mickey Mouse!

You will also see Tinker Bell, Genie, the Fairy Godmother, Rafiki, and even Elsa.

With unforgettable songs such as "Let it Go" and "Friend like Me", this is an unmissable spectacular. We think this is one of the best shows that Disneyland Paris has ever done - it is of West End theatre quality.

A "Secure Your Seat" option is available for €15 per person for this show if you don't want to wait and have a guaranteed seat.

Note: This show is on a scheduled break from 6 January to 20 April, 2025.

RC Racer

Hop on the RC car from Pixar's *Toy Story* films, and feel the wind in your hair as you ride both forwards and backwards along the track.

The ride is great fun and a good adrenaline rush – it is often compared to the swinging pirate ships found at many theme parks. However, here you are also secured by overhead harnesses.

☆ No	↕ 1.20m	📷 No	◷ 2 mins	⧗ 30 to 60 mins

You'll be 24m (80ft) up at the highest point, and the free-fall-like feeling backwards is great fun.

The ride *looks* more intense than it actually *is*, in our opinion.

RC Racer has one of the park's most slow-moving and tedious queues, so we would avoid it if waits are long.

Top Tip: A *Single Rider* queue allows guests to save time and board individually. Unusually, this *Single Rider* queue only starts halfway into the regular queue, so you may have to wait in the regular queue line for a long time until the split point.

Ride this early in the day as queues build up quickly.

Toy Soldiers Parachute Drop

Board one of the Toy Soldiers' parachutes and get ready to soar into the sky and glide back down to the ground again and again.

This is a great fun family ride.

☆ No	↕ 0.81m	📷 No	◷ 1 min	⧗ 45 to 75 mins

Queues can get extremely long for this ride, so get here early.

Top Tip: A *Single Rider* queue line is available for guests happy to board individually.

Slinky Dog Zigzag Spin

Hop on *Slinky Dog* and enjoy spinning round and round in circles getting increasingly faster and faster.

The ride is gentle enough for younger children but still provides a fun experience for guests of all ages.

☆ No	↕ None	📷 No	◷ 90 secs	⧗ 20 to 45 mins

Dining

Bistrot Chez Remy (€€€€ to €€€€€) – Table Service. Set menus only (€45 and €55 for adults, €30 for children). Advanced reservations are recommended as this is the only Table Service restaurant in the park so it books up quickly.

Avengers Campus

This is the newerst area of the park. In addition to the attractions below, you can also meet characters at the Hero Training Center.

Avengers Assemble: Flight Force

On this high-speed rollercoaster, guests team up with Iron Man, Captain Marvel and other superheroes to save the world.

You'll reach speeds of 92 km/h (57 mph) and can expect to go upside down several times on this ride.

This is easily the most thrilling ride at *Walt Disney Studios Park*.

☆ Yes   ↕ 1.20m   📷 Yes   ⏱ 90 secs   ⏳ 25 to 45 mins

Spider-Man W.E.B. Adventure

Unleash your inner superhero in this family-friendly attraction. On this 3D interactive ride, you'll use your hands to sling webs onto screens to collect Spider-Bots that have gone rogue and causing chaos in *Avengers Campus*.

As the park's newest ride, it typically has one of the longest waits in the park. You can use the *Single Rider* queue line to reduce this.

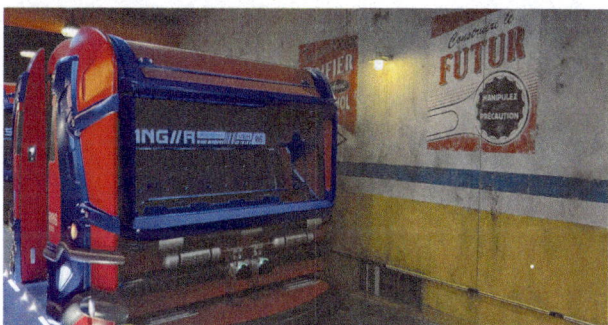

☆ Yes   ↕ None   📷 No   ⏱ 4 mins   ⏳ 60 to 90 mins

Dining
Stark Factory (€) – Counter Service. Serves pizzas, pasta and salads.
Super Diner (€) – Counter Service. Serves toasted sandwiches.
PYM Kitchen (€€€€) – Buffet serving American fare. €45 per adult and €25 per child.
There are also two food trucks. The **FAN-tastic Food Truck** (€) serves hot dogs and the **WEB Food Truck** (€) serves noodles.

Parades and Fireworks at Walt Disney Studios Park
Unfortunately, this park does not have a daytime or nighttime parade at the moment. However, the *Twilight Zone: Tower of Terror* becomes the backdrop for nighttime shows during seasonal events such as Christmas and New Year's Eve, as well as occasional extra special events throughout the year. Check the Disneyland Paris app for schedules.

Touring Plans

Touring plans are easy-to-follow guides that minimise your wait time in queue lines throughout the day. Following them lets you make the most of your time in the parks and experience more attractions. We have created several different touring plans available to suit your needs.

To see all of *Disneyland Park*, you will need to allocate at least two days. However, you can hit the headline attractions at the park in just one day if you are pressed for time. *Walt Disney Studios Park* can be comfortably seen in less than a day.

Unless you visit during the off-peak season, you will find it difficult to see the highlights from both parks in one day – there is not enough time.

These touring plans are not set in stone, so feel free to adapt them to your party's needs. The plans focus on experiencing the rides; if you want to focus on meeting all the characters or seeing all the shows, then these touring plans are unlikely to suit you. The only way to minimise waits for the characters is to get to the parks (and meet and greets) early.

These touring plans are intense, BUT you will get to see and do as much as possible during your visit. If you are at the resort for multiple days, feel free to follow the plans more leisurely. Also, if you do not want to experience a particular ride, skip that step but do not change the order of the steps.

If an attraction is closed for refurbishment during your trip, skip that step.

You must purchase your tickets in advance to make the most of your time and these touring plans.

Insider Tip: To minimise the time you spend waiting in queue lines, you will often need to cross the park from one side to the other. For example, the three roller coasters at *Disneyland Park* are all far away from each other – this is done to spread crowds more evenly.

Disneyland Park Touring Notes

Two attractions that are not covered in these plans:
• *Thunder Mesa Riverboat Landing* - The wait time for this attraction is never longer than 30 minutes (typically around 15 minutes), so you may be able to fit it in.
• *Disneyland Railroad* - This travels around the park. There are four different stations to board at; the one with the shortest wait is usually *Frontierland Station*, as it is the most hidden.

Be aware that both these attractions stop operation before the park closes.

Disneyland Paris also lists the following as attractions, so you might want to fit them in at some point:
• *Horse-Drawn Streetcars*
• *Main Street Vehicles*
• *The Liberty* and *Discovery Arcades*

We do not feel these are must-dos unless you have time to spare.

This guide does not take into account live shows, as those vary throughout the year, check the Disneyland Paris app for timings and try to find time to watch them.

Also, make sure to visit the *Gallery* inside *Sleeping Beauty Castle* (upstairs) and the *Dragon's Lair* underneath. Entry to *Sleeping Beauty Castle* ends at least one hour before *Disney Tales of Magic*, as does all of *Fantasyland*.

Disneyland Park
1 Day Plan for Guests with Extra Magic Time

Step 1: At 8:20am, be at the park gates for entry - the park opens at 8:30am. Make sure you have downloaded the Disneyland Paris app. This lists parade, show, character and firework times, and attraction closures. If you want to meet any characters, do this before the rides. Walk down *Main Street, U.S.A.,* get photos and head straight to *Sleeping Beauty Castle*.

Step 2: Enter *Fantasyland* and ride *Dumbo: The Flying Elephant* first, followed by *Peter Pan's Flight*.

Step 3: Head to *Frontierland* and ride *Big Thunder Mountain*.

Step 4: If it is not yet 9:15am, ride *Phantom Manor*. If it is 9:15am or later, enter Discoveryland and ride *Buzz Lightyear Laser Blast*.

Step 5: Ride *Orbitron - Machines Volantes*.

Step 6: The park will now be open to all guests. Ride *Autopia*.

Step 7: Ride *Star Wars Hyperspace Mountain*.

Step 8: Ride *Star Tours: L'Aventure Continue*.

Step 9: Visit *Les Mystères du Nautilus*.

Step 10: Time to visit *Fantasyland*. Here, ride *Les Voyages de Pinocchio* and *Blanche Neige et les Sept Nains*.

Step 11: Grab some lunch.

Step 12: You now have a few rides left to do in *Fantasyland*. Experience *Casey Junior, Le Pays des Contes de Fées, "it's a small world"* and *Le Carousel de Lancelot*. Ride these one after another, in any order you wish, if you want to do them all. *Casey Junior* and *Storybook Canal Boats* close several hours before the rest of the park.

Step 13: If any live shows such as *The Lion King* are playing during your visit, you should watch these now.

Step 14: Check the time of the parade, and grab a spot at least 45 minutes before the start time.

Step 15: Many guests leave the park after the parade, so it will now be less busy. This is the time to either have a bit of a rest on a bench to avoid burning out or to go on rides with fast-moving queues. Ride *Pirates of the Caribbean*.

Step 16: Ride *Indiana Jones et le Temple du Péril*.

Step 17: Now, depending on the time of the day, and when the park closes, it is either time to have dinner or do the walkthrough attractions.

Walkthrough attractions do not have a wait time and you can show up whenever you want. These include *Adventure Isle and La Cabane des Robinson, Le Passage Enchanté d'Aladdin* and *Alice's Curious Labyrinth*. Prioritise the labyrinth as it closes first.

Step 18: Grab a spot for *Disney Tales of Magic* at least 45 minutes before showtime. We like to enjoy a hot dog and fries from *Casey's Corner* while waiting for the show to begin.

1 Day Plan for Guests without Extra Magic Time - Focus: Kids Rides

Step 1: Arrive by 9:10am at *Disneyland Park*'s entrance. Enter the park when it opens at 9:30am.

Make sure you have downloaded the Disneyland Paris app. This contains parade, show, character and firework times, as well as attraction closures and park hours.

Step 2: Walk down *Main Street, U.S.A.*, get photos and proceed straight to *Sleeping Beauty Castle*. Come back later for photos.

Step 3: Ride *Peter Pan's Flight*.

Step 4: Ride *Dumbo the Flying Elephant*.

Step 5: Ride *Autopia*.

Step 6: Ride *Buzz Lightyear Laser Blast*.

Step 7: Have lunch.

Step 8: Ride *Casey Junior*.

Step 9: Ride *Le Pays des Contes de Fees* next.

Step 10: Ride *Pinocchio,* and *Snow White* in *Fantasyland*.

Step 11: Get a spot for the parade at least 45 minutes before the start time anywhere along the parade route. Check the app for the start time.

Step 12: Explore inside *Sleeping Beauty Castle*.

Step 13: Ride *"it's a small world"* in *Fantasyland*.

Step 14: Decision: *Explore Alice's Curious Labyrinth* or ride *Le Carousel de Lancelot*. If there is still a lot of time left until the park closes, feel free to do both.

Step 15: If any shows are playing, now is a great time to watch one.

Step 16: Ride *Pirates of the Caribbean* in *Adventureland*. Then visit *La Cabane des Robinsons* if it is still open at this time of day.

Step 17: Ride *Phantom Manor* in *Frontierland*.

Step 18: Have dinner.

Step 19: Grab a spot for *Disney Tales of Magic* at least 45 minutes before showtime. We like to grab a hot dog and fries from *Casey's Corner* and eat this while waiting for the show to begin.

Note: If your children want a thrill, *Big Thunder Mountain* in *Frontierland* should be your choice, as it does not go upside down and is the tamest roller coaster in the park.

1 Day Plan for Guests without Extra Magic Time - Focus: Thrills

Step 1: Arrive at 9:10am at the entrance to *Disneyland Park*. Enter when the park opens at 9:30am.

Make sure you have downloaded the Disneyland Paris app. This contains parade, show, character meeting and firework times, attraction closures and park hours.

Step 2: Walk down *Main Street, U.S.A.*, get photos and proceed straight to *Sleeping Beauty Castle*. Come back later for photos.

Step 3: Ride *Big Thunder Mountain* in *Frontierland* immediately when the park opens.

Step 4: Ride *Star Wars Hyperspace Mountain* in *Discoveryland*.

Step 5: Ride *Star Tours*.

Step 6: Ride *Indiana Jones et le Temple du Péril* in *Adventureland*. Now you have ridden all the roller coasters in this park.

Step 7: Ride *Pirates of the Caribbean*.

Step 8: Time for lunch.

Step 9: If you are interested in watching any shows such as *The Lion King*, now is the perfect time.

Step 10: Explore *Les Mystères du Nautilus* and other walkthroughs such as *Le Passage Enchanté d'Aladdin* or *La Cabane des Robinson*.

Step 11: Ride *"it's a small world"*.

Step 12: Get a spot for the parade at least 45 minutes before the start time anywhere along the parade route. Check the app for parade timings.

Step 13: Ride *Autopia*.

Step 14: Ride *Phantom Manor*.

Step 15: Ride *Peter Pan's Flight* and explore *Alice's Curious Labyrinth*.

Step 16: Have dinner.

Step 17: Grab a spot for *Disney Tales of Magic* at least 45 minutes before showtime. We like to grab a hot dog and fries from *Casey's Corner* and eat this while waiting for the show to begin.

2 Day Disneyland Park Touring Plan

If you want to experience everything *Disneyland Park* offers in two days, follow the 1-Day plan for 'Kids Rides' one day and the 1-Day plan for 'Thrill Rides' the next day. This will cover all the rides in the most logical sequence. Combine the touring plans with *Extra Magic Time* if you have that available, and you should be able to comfortably experience *Disneyland Park* and all its attractions.

If you have three days or longer at *Disneyland Park*, there is no need to follow our touring plans rigidly. Make sure to arrive early and visit the busiest rides at the start or end of the day, enjoying shows and walkthroughs in the middle of the day.

Walt Disney Studios Park

Step 1: Arrive at the *Walt Disney Studios Park* entrance by 9:10am. Enter the park when it opens at 9:30am.

Make sure you have downloaded the Disneyland Paris app before your visit. Walk through *Studio 1* briskly - you can return and look around this area later.

Step 2: Ride *Crush's Coaster*.

Step 3: Ride *Spider-Man W.E.B. Adventure*. There *will* be a queue for this ride but doing this now allows you to do the park's busiest ride *(Crush's Coaster)* with minimal wait.

Step 4: Visit *Toy Story Playland*. There are several attractions to experience here. Ride them in this order: *Toy Soldiers Parachute Drop*, *RC Racer* and *Slinky Dog*.

Step 5: Ride *Ratatouille: The Adventure*.

Step 6: Ride *Cars Quatre Roues Rallye* – this is located opposite *Crush's Coaster*.

Step 7: Ride *The Twilight Zone: Tower of Terror*.

Step 8: Experience *Animation Celebration* - check the schedule in your app.

Step 9: Ride *Cars Road Trip*.

Step 10: Ride *Flying Carpets over Agrabah*.

Step 11: Ride *Avengers Assemble: Flight Force*.

Step 12: Watch some of the park's shows.

Step 13: That is it for all the rides. This park is tiny in comparison to *Disneyland Park*.

As well as the character meets, there are three main shows left to experience, so take these in according to their schedules which are available in the app.

These shows are:
• *Stitch Live*
• *Mickey & The Magician*
• *Minnie's Musical Moment at Studio D*
• *TOGETHER: A Pixar Musical Adventure*
• *Alice & the Queen of Hearts: Back to Wonderland (returns Spring 2025)*
• *Doctor Strange: Mystery of the Mystics (until 29 March 2025)*

Important: Guests with *Extra Magic Time* access should follow this plan in the same order, skipping any rides which are closed during the early opening timeframe.

Outside the Parks

A trip to Disneyland Paris isn't just about the theme parks - there are many things to do outside the parks, such as the shopping district, Disney Village. Plus, the fun does not have to stop at the resort. After all, you are just outside one of Europe's largest and most vibrant cities. Plus, there are opportunities for shopping and other adventures nearby.

Disney Village

Disney Village is an entertainment district located next to the theme parks and on-site hotels where you can continue the fun after the parks close. This area houses a cinema, restaurants, shops, bars and more. Admission to *Disney Village* is free.

Entertainment
Panoramagique

Soar into the sky and get a bird's-eye view of Disneyland Paris from the world's largest helium-filled passenger balloon – *Panoramagique*.

This is a great way to take photos of the resort where you can see everything around you, including both theme parks, *Disney Village* and the resort hotels.

It truly is a unique perspective from which you can appreciate the scale of the resort.

Pricing is €20 per adult and €15 per child for the flight (free for children under 3). A slight discount is available for booking online.

Alternatively, you can take the "show flight" during the fireworks at *Disneyland Park* for €35 per adult and €25 per child.

Flights last 6 minutes and do not operate in high winds or adverse weather conditions. Visit panoramagique.com for live updates. The nighttime show flight lasts about 30 minutes.

La Marina

La Marina offers water activities from rowing to pedal boats, and electric boats to hydro bikes. Land-based activities are also available, such as surrey bikes which you can hire. Activities operate at a charge and are based on weather conditions.

Operating times are 16:00 to 22:00 daily during the high season (school holidays) and on weekends. Activities may also be available at other times.

Pricing:
• *Electric boat hire* – €20 for 20 minutes, 5 people maximum per boat
• *Hydro Bikes* – €5 for 20 minutes, 1 person per bike. Minimum age: 12.
• *Pedal Boats* – €10 for 20 minutes, 5 people maximum per boat.
• *Surrey bike* – €10 for 20 minutes for a 2-adult + 1 child bike, or €15 for 20 minutes for a 4-adult + 1 child bike.

More Entertainment

• **Sports Bar & Lounge** - Being at Disneyland Paris does not mean missing out on your favourite sporting events. Go to the *Sports Bar* and watch the game on the giant screen, while having a drink or two and a snack. *Sports Bar* also hosts weekly karaoke sessions and other live entertainment open to everyone at no cost. This location will reopen in 2025 as a reimagined and more upscale offering.

• **Billy Bob's** - As well as being a restaurant during the day, *Billy Bob's* is a bar and nightclub when the night draws in. Children are allowed in at all times of the day and night, except during some adult-only events. *Cast Members* often frequent the bar at the end of a hard day's work at the theme parks – here drinks are free-flowing and adults and children alike can dance the night away.

• **Cinema Gaumont** - With 15 different auditoriums, including one with an IMAX screen, there is bound to be something for you to enjoy watching at this cinema. You can check film schedules in advance at http://bit.ly/dlpcinema. Films listed as VOST (usually only one) are shown in their original language with French subtitles.

Dining

Dining Key:
€ (Under €16)
€€ (€16 to €29)
€€€ (€30 to €39)
€€€€ (€40 to €49)
€€€€€ (€50+)

Prices relate to set menus for one person where available.

Most restaurants at *Disney Village* do not accept Meal Plans unless otherwise stated.

Disney Village has a variety of dining options, from Quick/Counter Service (fast food) to more traditional Table Service restaurants.

McDonald's (€) – Counter Service. *McDonald's* needs no introduction as a fast-food chain, but this branch has higher prices than usual due to the location. A standard meal costs between €9 and €12, with a child's meal costing about €4.50. Be aware that queues can be long if you do not use the touch screens and want to order from an employee instead. The screens can be set to English easily and accept bank cards but not cash; we highly recommend using these.

Starbucks Coffee (€) – Counter Service. This is a standard *Starbucks* location.

However, it should be noted that *Starbucks* is not cheap in France, and this location is no exception. A hot or cold brewed drink is priced between €5 and €7.50, and sandwiches are about €6.50.

Earl of Sandwich (€) – Counter Service. Prices are

€9-9.50 for a "gourmet" heated sandwich and €9 for a salad. Pizzas are €13.50. A kids' set menu is €9.

Annette's Diner (€€ to €€€) [Accepts Meal Plans] – Table Service. The American-style breakfast menu is €17 and is served daily until 11:30am. Milkshakes are €12.50.

The Royal Pub (€€ to €€€) – Table Service. Serves mainly English pub-style food. There is also a happy hour and an all-day breakfast.

Rainforest Cafe (€€ to €€€)– Table Service with a unique rainforest-like ambience.

The Steakhouse [Accepts Meal Plans] (€€€ to €€€€€) – Table Service with set menus and a la carte dishes - including, surprisingly, several vegetarian options.

Billy Bob's Country Western Saloon – Billy Bob's is divided into two dining establishments – **Bar Snacks** (€), a snack and Quick Service location, and **La Grange** (€€€€) [Accepts Meal Plans], an all-you-can-eat Tex Mex buffet.

Brasserie Rosalie (€€ to €€€€) – Table Service inspired by a traditional French brasserie with a terrace looking over Lake Disney. A 2-course weekday lunch menu is €19.50; the all-day adults menu is €40 and kids menu is €16. A la carte is also available and there is an extensive wine list.

There is also a takeaway bakery area selling pastries, sandwiches and salads. A takeaway breakfast meal is €4.50, and a sandwich lunch meal is €13.

Sports Bar (€ to €€) – Counter Service and Snacks. Sandwiches, burgers, pasta bolognese, hot dogs, fish and chips, and pizzas. This location is currently under refurbishment and due to reopen in 2025.

Vapiano (€) – Table service with fresh food. Pick a seat, then order your pizza or pasta with a QR code, it's made fresh and is delivered in minutes. No set menus; main courses are €14 to €19.

Five Guys (€) – Counter service. The best burgers at Disneyland Paris, in our opinion. Expect to pay €11 to €14 for a burger. Fries and drinks are extra.

Shopping

After a meal, you may want to treat yourself to some retail therapy; here you are spoilt for choice with several merchandise locations.

World of Disney – As you walk into *Disney Village* from the parks, this is the first store you see. *World Of Disney* is the best place to get your Disney merchandise outside of the theme parks. It is also the largest store at the resort, featuring a beautiful interior and a good selection of merchandise.

Disney Store – This classic location is a traditional-style Disney store. Uniquely, here you can create your own lightsabers and Potato Head figures, as well as choose from a selection of more common Disney merchandise. This store will be refurbished in 2025 and become Disney Wonders.

Three other new concept stores will be opening in the first quarter of 2025:
- **Disney Style**: a lifestyle/fashion destination
- **Disney Glamour**: featuring fashion brands collabs

- **Deco by Disney:** home decoration and Art on Demand

LEGO Store – This is the largest LEGO store in France. It features all kinds of different LEGO sets, but unfortunately, it does not feature any exclusive Disney-themed merchandise. Nevertheless, it is worth a visit for fans of the colourful bricks.

Rainforest Café Store – The perfect place to get all your *Rainforest Café* branded merchandise.

Paris

Disneyland Paris is a mere 35 minutes away from the centre of Paris by train, so visiting the 'City of Lights' should be considered on an extended trip.

Paris is filled with monuments, museums, rich culture and history. You should try to visit some of the following world-class attractions during your time in the city such as the Eiffel Tower, *Musée du Louvre, Musée d'Orsay, Arc de Triomphe, Champs Elysées, Montmartre* and the *Sacre Coeur* church.

Museums are generally reasonably priced, and European Economic Area citizens (the UK is not included) aged under 26 get free entry to most museums in the city. Plus, all visitors under the age of 18 get free entry with ID. There are even monthly openings of the museums with free admission for everyone, regardless of age.

We recommend taking a cruise on the river Seine or a bus tour, which will allow you to see several monuments in one go while on the move.

If you wish to visit several attractions and get unlimited public transport, the *Paris Pass* is worth considering.

To get to central Paris, catch the RER A line train from *Marne-la-Vallee – Chessy* station, located just a two-minute walk from the parks. Once you are in the centre of Paris, you can use the metro to get around.

A 1-day pass is the best travel ticket (priced at €12for zones 1 to 5, plus €2 for the *Navigo* card - this ticket is also available on your smartphone via the *Bonjour RATP* app). It allows unlimited travel for one day until midnight on the transport system within the Paris region, including to

and from Disneyland Paris. Alternatively if you are only want the journey into Paris and will then walk around - one-way tickets are available for €2.50 on the RER.

Disneyland Paris sells several excursions to Paris:

Paris Essentials – A free-style tour with time to explore alone. It includes a return coach trip from Disneyland Paris and a river cruise in Paris. Prices are about €55 per adult and €45 per child.

Versailles & Paris Tour – Return coach transport from Disneyland Paris, entry to Versailles Palace, transfer to the city centre, and a river cruise.

Other tour options are also available from €69 per person.

Val d'Europe

Located minutes away from Disneyland Paris is *Val d'Europe* - a town designed by Disney with a huge shopping centre and outlet mall.

It is only one stop away from Disney on the RER A line train (€2.50 per adult/ €1.25 per child). Trains run every 10 minutes with a journey time of about 2 minutes.

You can also walk in about 25 minutes.

If using the RER train, make sure to leave *Val d'Europe* station through the exit marked *Centre Commercial*.

Outside the station, turn right and walk straight ahead, crossing the road.

The shopping centre will be in front of you. Shops are open from 10:00am until 8:30pm on Monday to Saturday (and close at 8:00pm on Sunday), with restaurants staying open until midnight daily. Note that it is closed on some public holidays.

If you would like to stock up on groceries, there is a huge *Auchan* supermarket in the shopping centre, as well as a *SeaLife* aquarium (entry is €24 per person, cheaper online), and hundreds of stores.

You can also follow the signs to *La Vallée Village* for an excellent outlet village with designer luxury goods at reduced prices.

Center Parcs Villages Nature Paris

Villages Nature is located 15 minutes from the main Disneyland Paris site.

This eco-tourism location was built around a geothermal lagoon. It features apartment-style accommodation, numerous restaurants to enjoy and recreation options.

A public bus runs between *Villages Nature* and Disneyland Paris, and you can book accommodation packages to stay at *Villages Nature* and play at Disneyland Paris. This bus service is paid.

Aqua Mundo (an indoor water park) features giant water slides, a wave pool, and an outdoor lagoon heated to 30 degrees Celcius year-round. This is open daily from 10:00am to 7-8:00pm.

Also on offer: educational programs and workshops, four landscaped gardens inspired by the four elements, a huge outdoor playground, tree-climbing trails, a bowling alley, boutiques, an escape room. cultural events and much more.

If you are not staying at the accommodation, you can buy a day pass to visit this unique location for €35 to €50 per adult and €15 to €35 per child. On certain days you can also buy a half-day pass which allows access from 4:00pm to 11:00pm from €25 per adult and €15 per child. Parking is an extra €10. You can book this day ticket at centerparcs.eu under "Day Visit".

Accommodation starts at around €300 for 2 nights - please note Disneyland Paris admission tickets are not included when staying here and this is not an official Disney hotel. Tickets are included if you book this accommodation via Disneyland Paris.

Davy Crockett's Adventure

If you like adventure assault courses, you will love *Davy Crockett's Adventure!* There are swings, trapezes, rope bridges, ladders and much more to explore, making this High Rope location excellent family fun.

This attraction is located at the *Disney's Davy Crockett Ranch* entrance – a campsite run by Disneyland Paris and considered one of the seven on-site hotels. It is 8km from the central resort hub.

This activity is open seasonally – visit www.aventure-aventure.com for opening times (Under 'Préparer ma visite' and then 'Calandrier'). The ropes courses are operated by a third-party company and not Disneyland Paris.

Expect to pay €25 to €29 per person for those 140cm or taller, and €18 to €22 for those between 110cm and 139cm. Those under 110cm (3 to 5 years) pay €13-€15.

Spectator tickets are available for €8 each, though they are included with child tickets.

Tickets should be purchased online before visiting.

Note there is no shuttle bus to *Disney's Davy Crockett, Ranch* where this activity is located. You will need a car to participate in the experience, or you can book a taxi.

Guests with Disabilities

Disneyland Paris is designed to be enjoyed by everyone, regardless of their mental or physical abilities. Over 60,000 guests with disabilities visit the resort each year.

Accessibility Cards

If you have a guest with an officially recognised disability in your party, stop by the Disney Hotels front desks or the dedicated desks at the entrance to either park on the first day of your visit. Alternatively, you can start the process in advance online at bit.ly/prioritydlp.

If you have visited Disneyland Paris before and used the system, please note it was radically overhauled in late 2021.

Guests who have a disability can apply for one of two cards that will facilitate their visit: the *Priority Card* and the *Easy Access Card*.

Both cards have a photo of the holder and a QR code to confirm validity.

The **Priority Card** allows a permanently disabled guest and up to 4 members of

their party access to attractions via a specially adapted entrance. This entrance will involve less walking and no stairs. It could be through the ride's exit, the *Disney Premier Access* entrance or a specially adapted queue line. In cases where the standard queue line is adapted, you will use the standard access. Entry procedures vary from ride to ride – to learn the boarding options available at each attraction, ask a *Cast Member* at the ride entrance.

The *Priority Card* provides priority but not *instant* access; wait times vary based on the number of people in the *Priority Card* queue. To receive the card, the disabled person (or their helper) must present an official document issued by the local government or medical authorities from

any country. A medical certificate is *not* sufficient. Proof of ID is required and may be requested when boarding rides.

Valid supporting documentation to prove disability varies greatly between countries and we recommend checking bit.ly/prioritydlp for the full list.

The **Easy Access Card** is for guests with a recognised Long Term Chronic Disease. The full list of 30 eligible illnesses can be seen at bit.ly/easyaccessdlp. Examples vary from a debilitating stroke to diabetes, and leprosy to cystic fibrosis.

You'll need an original medical certificate in French or English signed and stamped by a medical doctor and less than 3 months old, indicating the long-term chronic disease.

This card can only be obtained at Disneyland Paris and not in advance - you can do this at Guest Services at the entrance to the parks or at your hotel's front desk.

This card does not offer priority access. Instead, you will present the card at an attraction entrance, receive a time-slot reservation to return and then can enter the ride at that time, bypassing the regular queue line. You can only make one ride reservation at a time.

This card is valid for the named guest plus up to 4 members of their party.

Additional information: When a person with a disability asks for a *Priority Card*, they are asked

questions to determine which rides will be accessible to them. For example, someone who cannot transfer out of a wheelchair cannot ride *Pirates of the Caribbean*.

As well as the card itself, you will be given a copy of the Accessibility Guide with detailed information on each attraction. You can also consult this in advance at www.bit.ly/dlpdisab before your trip.

Some attractions require guests with either card to make a reservation at the ride entrance and return later. Organised character meet-and-greets usually use a reservation system, and there will be a *Cast Member* with the characters to

reserve a slot for you.

Some attractions may not be accessible to guests with certain disabilities. In this case, family members cannot use the card in place of the disabled person – they must use the standby queue or can choose to pay for *Disney Premier Access*, if available.

Expectant mothers can get a bracelet that acts similarly to the *Easy Access Card* at their Disney hotel or *Guest Relations* at either park. A medical certificate dated within the last 3 months in English or French is required. You can be accompanied by 4 people for the attractions and shows, and 2 for the parades.

Services for Guests with Disabilities

Hearing-impaired visitors: Disney Park information points, many cash desks, all park theatres, and some *Walt Disney Studios Park* attractions, are equipped with induction loops to assist guests.

Mobility-impaired visitors: *Cast Members* cannot escort or help disabled guests to attractions. They will, of course, provide directions and assist inside attractions.

Some attractions require that disabled guests transfer from their wheelchairs to an attraction vehicle. For these attractions, disabled guests must be accompanied by at least one non-disabled adult (18+) to assist. *Cast Members* cannot help visitors in or out of their wheelchairs or ride vehicles.

For some attractions, visitors must be ambulatory.

In *Walt Disney Studios Park*, all attraction queues are wheelchair accessible; this is also true for *Buzz Lightyear Laser Blast, Princess Pavilion* and *Meet Mickey Mouse* in Disneyland Park. The *Priority Card* allows guests entry via a separate entrance for attractions where this is not the case.

Designated viewing areas are available for guests in wheelchairs for the daily parade, *Disney Tales of Magic* and stage shows.

All toilets have accessible areas for visitors with reduced mobility.

Unisex toilets (with cubicles

so a carer may join wheelchair users) are available in every land of *Disneyland Park*.

All shops and Table Service restaurants are accessible. At Quick Service places, ask a *Cast Member* for assistance if necessary.

An accessible shuttle bus is available between all Disney hotels (except *Disney's Davy Crockett Ranch)* and the theme parks. Ask at the hotel desk, the *Disney Express* desk at *Marne La Vallée – Chessy* station, or Guest Services in the parks for details and to book this free service.

All Disney Hotels have rooms adapted to meet the needs of guests in wheelchairs. These have an extra-large bathroom with a bath, handrails and a raised toilet. Additionally, mobility-impaired guests can borrow a seat to help them wash without assistance (to be requested when making the reservation).

The bedroom door has a spy hole at wheelchair height in accessible rooms. Bathrooms at *Disney's Davy Crockett Ranch, Sequoia Lodge* and *Santa Fe* Hotels have a shower suitable for mobility-impaired guests.

Visually impaired guests:
An app called *AudioSpot*, available on iOS and Android, describes surroundings, attractions, and food menus in audio form.

A companion may need to describe the surroundings in some areas of the park. Some attractions and areas of the park are dimly lit.

At hotels, Disney recommends that visually impaired guests inform the hotel reception of their visual impairment upon arrival. A *Cast Member* will show guests to their room, and show them around the rest of the hotel so that visually impaired guests can orientate themselves.

Telephones and TV remotes with large buttons, as well as room keys with Braille, may be requested when making a reservation or at reception upon arrival.

Guide Dogs:
Guide and assistant dogs are allowed in the parks and at certain attractions. Dogs must be left with a helper at attractions where dogs are not permitted. Dogs may not be left unattended or with a *Cast Member*.

Visually impaired guests may need to be accompanied on certain attractions. If bringing a guide dog, there must be at least two helpers with a disabled guest – one to accompany the guest and another to stay with the guide dog.

Food Allergies:
Disneyland Paris offers allergen-free meals at selected restaurants. We recommend alerting your hotel so an allergen-free breakfast can be prepared. When booking Table Service meals, state your allergies. Review Disneyland Paris' allergen guide at www.bit.ly/dlpallergy.

Other information:
Cast Members may refuse guests access to attractions for safety reasons.

Some attractions only accept one guest with disabilities at a time for safety and legal reasons. In these cases, the wait for these guests can be as long or longer than the standard queue line.

Guests with medication that must be kept cool may leave this at one of the First Aid points in the two theme parks or *Disney Village*.

For safety reasons, all visitors with reduced mobility or a visual impairment, a cognitive or mental health disorder, a behavioural disorder or autism, or a learning disability, are recommended to be accompanied by at least one non-disabled companion over the age of 18 to assist them. This is not compulsory, but Disneyland Paris recommends this for a guest's first visit.

Some attractions may have low-light areas, flashing lights or loud sound effects, moving floors and other effects. Companions should pay particular attention to all these factors when preparing for their stay. They should read the safety information available at the entrance to each attraction and the Disney Parks Accessibility Guide.

Ticket discounts:
Guests with a disability (and one accompanying person) are entitled to a 25% discount on park tickets and annual passes.

An official document issued by your local government or medical authorities from any country will be accepted as proof of disability. A medical certificate will not be sufficient.

These discounted tickets can be purchased at a Disney hotel, the park entrances at dedicated desks or online (proof must be shown when picking up).

Disneyland Paris for Walt Disney World Regulars

Many guests visit Disneyland Paris after visiting the Walt Disney World Resort in Florida. Both resorts immerse you in the Disney magic, but it is important to understand that the two locations are very different. This chapter helps you compare and contrast.

The Cast Members and Languages

The *Cast Members* in Florida and California, mostly give you American-style customer service, go above and beyond, are incredibly polite, have a passion for Disney and do everything to make your stay as magical as possible.

However, the *Cast Members* in the US are restricted by the Disney rulebook, which even affects their personal lives, such as how they can cut and style their hair.

Disneyland Paris is a Disney Park for the 21st century in a country where a *Disney Look* dictating employees' personal appearance is illegal. French employment laws are stringent, so *Cast Members* cannot be reprimanded for not smiling or for leaning at work.

Also, French customer service is very different from that in the USA. Having said this, most of the Disneyland Paris *Cast Members* are pleasant, inviting and helpful – however, do not expect American-style customer service in France.

All *Cast Members* must speak at least two major European languages, one of which must be French. Almost the entire *Cast* speak English well, but it is not mandatory.

On rare occasions, you may encounter a *Cast Member* who does not speak English, so it pays to learn some basic French. A *Bonjour, s'il vous plaît* or a *Merci* goes a long way in France.

Weather

Florida is known as the "sunshine state", and you can expect daily high temperatures to reach 30°C (80-90°F) for much of the year - especially in the summer. There are occasional cold snaps when the temperature drops for a few days, but nothing to the levels seen in Paris.

Paris' weather is much more variable; the average daily high in Paris in July and August is about 25°C (77°F), whereas temperatures in January and February have lows of 3°C (37°F) on average, often dipping below freezing.

In the summer, it is common for a few days to exceed 37°C (100°F) in Paris each year, whereas Florida rarely gets this warm.

Visitors to Walt Disney World have to deal with Hurricane season for half of the year (June to November) when the weather can be extreme, and hurricanes are possible. These are extremely uncommon in Paris.

Orlando visitors also deal with a tropical climate with daily thunderstorms in the summer, closing all outdoor attractions and drenching anyone unprepared for the weather. Paris' rain is more unpredictable and is present year-round, but thunderstorms are rare.

Local Customs

According to the latest figures from Disneyland Paris, around half of visitors to the resort were French before the Covid-19 pandemic, and 16% were from the UK. Other countries with a high number of guests include Spain and Italy. Disneyland Paris has a high proportion of European visitors, unlike Walt Disney World.

Many American customs do not apply to a European audience. For example, many Europeans do not queue in daily life. Instead, people gather in small groups instead of in an orderly queue. So, when a bus arrives, it is a free-for-all and people rush for the doors with no regard for those waiting for the longest.

During random character appearances in the parks, you can expect a crowd of parents pushing their children to get their photos taken first. When a queue is set up, though, Europeans do comply.

Tipping is also different. Meals in France have a service charge included in the price, so there is no need to tip (although a small tip is appreciated). This compares to the US, where tips of 20% of a meal's price are expected.

In general, guests are less respectful at the Parisian parks – they enter closed-off areas, sit anywhere they want, and smoke in the parks despite it being banned in most areas.

Guests in Europe also often expect to have an alcoholic beverage with their meal – as such, you will find beer on sale at Quick Service locations. Wine and other alcoholic drinks are also offered at all Table Service locations. The sale of alcoholic drinks has *not* harmed the parks' family-friendly atmosphere.

Lastly, the European audience is slightly more fashion-conscious than the crowds visiting Florida. Ponchos, for example, are sold at Disneyland Paris, but they are often replaced by umbrellas and raincoats instead.

Resort Size and Transportation

The size difference between the two resorts is staggering: Walt Disney World is 40 square miles or 103 square kilometres. In comparison, Disneyland Paris is a fifth of the size at 22.3 square kilometres.

From the furthest resort hotels to the parks is a 20-minute walk at Disneyland Paris or a 5-minute bus journey. However, at Walt Disney World, few journeys can be walked - not only because of the distance but because there are no pavements connecting most areas due to the resort's sprawling size and American car dependency.

At Disneyland Paris, the two theme parks are within

walking distance, as is *Disney Village*. Everything is at least one bus journey away from everything else at Walt Disney World.

The advantage of Disneyland Paris' small size is that you can walk across the whole resort, visit the other hotels easily, and spend less time travelling and more time enjoying yourself. The disadvantage is that there are fewer things to do: no water parks, fewer hotels, and, crucially, fewer theme parks (two in Paris versus four in Florida).

Looking at the theme parks, *Disneyland Park* is slightly bigger than *Magic Kingdom Park*, but with emptier, quieter areas and fewer rides. Park walkways feel much less crowded in Paris.

Walt Disney Studios Park in Paris is about half the size of *Disney's Hollywood Studios* in Orlando. The resort hotels in Paris are also generally smaller than their Floridian counterparts.

In fact, Disneyland Paris is much more comparable to the Disneyland Resort in California, where everything is within walking distance. However, Disneyland Paris is still *much* larger than the Disneyland Resort.

The area where Disneyland Paris is located is as much a major transport hub, as it is a world-class theme park resort. Just two minutes from the park entrances, you can hop on a high-speed train to travel across Europe.

Alternatively, you can use the local trains and travel into central Paris in just 35 minutes. You can also drive and be at non-Disney locations in just a few minutes too.

Disneyland Paris is all very self-contained, so if you do fancy escaping the magic, it is easy to do - unlike in Florida! For some people, this is a benefit, but others prefer the Floridian immersion of the Disney magic that lets them forget about the outside world.

Pricing

Disney trips can be very pricey.

At Disneyland Paris, room prices at on-site hotels include tickets to the theme parks for the length of stay. However, you will not find a room at a Disney hotel for under €330 ($350) per night for 2 people – and these are the cheapest rooms during off-peak seasons.

In contrast, the cheapest hotels in Walt Disney World are less than half this price, *but*, crucially, park tickets are not included.

A undated one-day entry ticket to Disneyland Paris for one park is €119 (£99 or $126) for adults and €111 for children. A two-park ticket is €144 ($152). The daily rate drastically reduces the longer you visit the resort. A 2-park, 4-day ticket for adults is €255-461 ($279-$487).

For comparison, at Walt Disney World, a one-day, one-park adult ticket is $116 to $201 depending on the date and park you are visiting, or a park hopper (for four theme parks) is $196 to $268. A 4-day ticket is $485-$673 for one park per day, or $575-$774 with the park hopper option).

Walt Disney World tickets are much more expensive. Although there are more activities in the Floridian parks, the 4-day hopper costs roughly twice as much per person. Plus, of course, the Paris ticket prices are not relevant if staying on-site as the tickets are included in your hotel cost.

Longer stays of 7 or 14 days at Walt Disney World become more affordable per day.

Food prices at Disneyland Paris are comparable to those in the US.

At Disneyland Paris, a burger, fries and drink combo will set you back about €17 ($18). A burger and fries in the US costs

about $14.50 without a drink or about $19.30 with one. With tax, the price is around $21 so Paris' food is slightly cheaper.

At Table Service locations, the price difference is more notable, however they are still close. A Set Menu at a decent in-park restaurant will set you back €45 to €55 ($50 to $60) at Disneyland Paris. The equivalent at Walt Disney World would be about 20% cheaper, but you need to add on a tip and tax bringing it to a similar amount.

Food-wise, don't expect signature foods like Dole Whips and Mickey Premium Bars in Disneyland Paris, either - or snacks in general, as snacking is less of a concept in Europe.

Skip-the-line systems

At Disneyland Paris, if you want to skip the standby queues at rides, you can use *Disney Premier Access* - you pay for this service individually for each ride.

At Walt Disney World, you can pay $20 to $39 per day to skip the queue for several rides at each park with *Lightning Lane MultiPass*. However, the top 2 rides in each park are not included. They cost an extra fee, just like Paris' Disney *Premier Access system*.

Both systems are digital and run on a smartphone app.

The previously free *Fastpass* system no longer exists at either resort.

Unique Attractions and Details

Disneyland Paris has many unique rides and shows which cannot be found at Walt Disney World.

In Disneyland Park, *Phantom Manor* is a beautiful reimagining of the classic *Haunted Mansion* ride with a new storyline and an entirely different interior but keeping many familiar scenes.

Pirates of the Caribbean is much longer, has a better queue, new scenes and bigger drops in Paris.

Star Wars Hyperspace Mountain is beautiful in Paris - it is an intense looping roller coaster that blows all the other *Space Mountain* rides out of the water; *Big Thunder Mountain* is more intense and fun in Paris, and is set in the middle of an island.

Furthermore, there are many unique walkthroughs such as *Nautilus* and *Alice's Curious Labyrinth*. *Casey Junior* and *Storybook Canal Boats* also do not exist in Florida.

Indiana Jones et le Temple du Péril is also a unique roller coaster. There is, however, no 'New Fantasyland expansion' in Paris.

The *Disney Tales of Magic* night-time spectacular is not too dissimilar to Magic Kingdom's *Happily Ever After*, although Paris' show is more high-tech.

In *Walt Disney Studios Park*, *Crush's Coaster* is a unique spinning roller coaster in the dark, and *Cars Quatre Roues Rallye* is a tea-cup style ride themed to the film *Cars*. *Cars Road Trip* is unique too.

Toy Story Playland has three unique rides, and *Animagique Theatre* is home to a unique stage show. *Stitch Live* is a cool interactive show, similar to *Turtle Talk with Crush*.

Finally, *Avenger's Campus* has two completely unique rides that Florida does not have, although *Avengers Assemble: Flight Force* is essentially a rethemed version of Florida's *Rock 'n' Roller Coaster*.

Disneyland Park is beautiful. Everything is incredibly elaborately themed, sharing inspiration from the American parks while introducing elements that cannot be found elsewhere.

In comparison, the theming in *Walt Disney Studios Park* is still sparse and leaves a lot to be desired.

Although over the past five years, there has been an effort to improve the park, *Walt Disney Studios Park* lacks the detail that makes Disney theme parks unique.

Even *Disney's Hollywood Studios*, which is (in our opinion) the worst-themed park at Walt Disney World, has superior theming to the *Studios* park in Paris. The *Avengers Campus* expansion has helped, but it is the upcoming (2026) *World of Frozen* area that will really improve this park.

The hotels at Disneyland Paris are American-themed but do not live up to the resort hotels found at Walt Disney World. The hotels in Paris are just hotels, whereas you could spend several days at the hotel resorts in the US and enjoy the surroundings and experiences on offer.

The Seasons and The Future

Disneyland Paris offers its guests something different throughout the year, with seasonal and special events that celebrate traditions such Halloween and Christmas. This section explores all of these. Plus, we take a look at the future of the resort.

Disney Music Festival

19th April to 7th September 2025

This brand new season for 2025 will feature *Minnie's Marching Band* where Minnie and her Marching Band stroll along *Main Street, U.S.A* playing Disney classics!

Moana and her musicians will also be in the park, and a new show called *Disney Music Hits Concert* will entertain guests of all ages.

Disneyland Paris Magical Pride

June

Celebrate the magic of diversity and show your pride with this after-hours LGBT-focused event at Disneyland Paris.

The event will feature an exclusive parade, live performances by famous artists, the chance to ride some of the most popular attractions late into the night, appearances by favourite Disney characters and much more.

Disneyland Paris has not confirmed if this event will be returning in 2025 at the time of publication.

Disney's Halloween Festival

October and Early November

Disneyland Paris' Halloween season is one of the most elaborate celebrations at the resort, with unique shows, parades, décors and more to delight guests.

The Halloween event is broadly similar each year, but some elements may not return for the 2025 season, and new bits may be added. This information is for 2024's Halloween season as it is too far to know what the season in 2025 will look like.

Disney usually releases specific details about six weeks before the Halloween season starts.

Decorations, Food and Merchandise – *Frontierland* is invaded by ghostly decorations for some great photo opportunities. Disney characters also sport Halloween-themed costumes. Villains-themed merchandise and special Halloween-inspired menus are available, as well as decorations at the on-site hotels. Plus, you'll also see other themed touches on *Main Street, U.S.A* and other areas of the park.

Character Meets – Keep your eyes peeled for meet and greets with Disney characters in their Halloween best.

Mickey's Halloween Celebration Parade – Treat yourself to Mickey's tricks as he steals the show on a fabulous *Phantom Manor* float in the wickedly wonderful Halloween Cavalcade. Souls of all ages will get in the spirit as Disney Characters parade along the streets of *Disneyland Park* in eye-popping autumn attire. You're sure to be spellbound!

On the 31st October 2024, Disney included an enhanced offering of entertainment for one evening only (including a special fireworks display) - and higher ticket prices for admission on this day. This was not a separately ticketed event - however, in previous years Disney has offered an after-hours Party event. As of late 2024, it has not been announced if this will be returning in 2025, so we have included the information below just in case.

Disney's Halloween Party (unconfirmed for 2025): Note this event did not happen in 2024. The information *may* be relevant in case it returns in 2025.

On the 31st of October between 8:30pm and 2:00am, this ticketed event offers an evening of frightening entertainment.

Unique entertainment is available during the party including character meet and greets, special shows and plenty of exclusive party-only entertainment.

Most *Disneyland Park* attractions are open during the event and guests may wear Halloween costumes (subject to restrictions).

Entry in previous years was €79 to €89 for guests aged 3 and up. Under 3s go free. Guests may enter the park from 5:00pm with party tickets.

Christmas

Mid-November to Early January

For the most magical time of the year, make Disneyland Paris your stop. Here you are guaranteed snow every day, magical characters and unforgettable experiences.

Traditionally, the Christmas seasons do not change hugely from year to year, so you can expect much of this information to be valid for the 2025 Christmas season too. Information on the 2025 season will be unveiled by Disney in September 2025 at the earliest, so the following details are based on the 2024 Christmas season.

The park will be filled with Christmas touches everywhere you go but no more so than *Main Street, U.S.A.* - here you will find a giant 24-metre Christmas tree, snowmen on each corner and baubles and tinsel abound.

Show: "Let's Sing Christmas!" – Get into the Christmas spirit and sing along with Mickey, Minnie, Donald, Daisy and Goofy in the magical *Let's Sing Christmas*!

Mickey's Dazzling Christmas Parade – This Christmas-themed parade marches down *Fantasyland* and *Main Street, U.S.A* twice a day. The parade stars Father Christmas until Christmas day. A mini-show stop takes place on Central Plaza in front of the castle.

Disney Princesses Holiday Season Celebration - Aurora, Cinderella, Belle, Tiana, Jasmine, Rapunzel, Ariel and Snow White amaze kids and grown-ups, with an elegant waltz at the foot of Sleeping Beauty Castle.

Christmas Tree Lighting – This has taken a few

different forms over the years. In previous years, the park's signature Christmas tree has come to life with the help of Mickey, Minnie and Santa in an illumination ceremony that was advertised as its own show. In 2024, the Christmas tree was lit up just before or after the parade but show times were not published, so you may wish to watch the parade from the Town Square area to catch both events.

Meet the Characters – Meet both Santa and Mickey at *Meet Mickey Mouse*. There are two queue lines – one for Mickey photos and the other for Santa photos. You'll also have the chance to meet Marie from the Aristocats, Scrooge McDuck, Thumper, Miss Bunny and more throughout the park!

Special Dinners – Christmas Eve and New Year's Eve dinners are big family affairs in Europe. As such, dinners on these days are available for a heavy supplement.

Prices vary from €75 to €230 per adult for Christmas Eve and New Year's Eve meals.

Full details on these meals are available over the phone and on the Disneyland Paris website.

We think these prices are exorbitant, with a family of 4 spending anywhere from €300 to €1000 on a single meal. We recommend eating at one of the Quick Service restaurants to avoid these hefty price tags (or at a Table Service location as a late lunch).

Alternatively, choose from one of the Table Service restaurants that do not offer special dinners, or eat at *Disney Village* at selected restaurants. Reservations are necessary many weeks in advance as these will sell out.

New Year's Eve

31st December

Celebrate the start of the New Year at Disneyland Paris.

This is traditionally the busiest day at the resort and you can expect the theme parks to reach maximum capacity with very long wait times for all rides.

Tickets for the 31st December 2024 were already sold out in early December.

The exact details of this evening has changed multiple times over the years.

All the Christmas entertainment is still running on this date and continues into early January.

In 2024, *Walt Disney Studios Park* is open until 10:00pm.

Disneyland Park is open until 1:00am with a special fireworks display and countdown for midnight.

Ticket prices are higher for this day and you can expect extra entertainment such as DJ parties on this special evening.

In previous years, Disneyland Park closed early and then had an after-hours party for an extra charge but we do not expect this to return.

The Future - Projects in Progress & Rumours

Walt Disney Studios Park Expansion – *Walt Disney Studios Park* is set to continue expanding in size, and with additional attractions - Disney is investing €2 billion into the theme park in total.

Construction began several years ago and the project is opening in phases. Still to come is:
• A new 'Studio 1' entrance area to the theme park
• A rebranding of the theme park from *Walt Disney Studios Park* to *Disney Adventure World*
• A brand new *World of Frozen* area with a lagoon, shops, a new grand avenue and a new boat ride.
• A minor spinning attraction *(Rapunzel's Tangled Spin)* on the new pathway to the lagoon and a dining location overlooking the lagoon *(Regal View Restaurant)*.
• A new nighttime spectacular on the lagoon in front of *World of Frozen*.
• A *Lion King* area with a water ride (likely beyond 2030).

You can see the concept art for this expansion area below.

Disney Village Expansion – *Disney Village* will expand and be updated over the coming years, with new shopping and dining experiences. The first of these was *Brasserie Rosalie*. A new Italian restaurant *(Casa Giulia)* will also open at the entrance to Disney Village replacing the now-closed Planet Hollywood.

Hotels – Disneyland Paris has been refurbishing its hotels over the past decade. The *Disneyland Hotel* reopened in January 2024. *Disney's Sequoia Lodge Hotel* is expected to undergo a multi-year refurbishment starting in late 2025 - it will not close during these works; they will be phased in instead.

A Special Thanks

Thank you very much for reading our travel guide. We hope this book has made a big difference to your trip to Disneyland Paris, and that you have found some tips that will save you time, money and hassle! Remember to take this guide with you when you are visiting the resort. This guide is also available in a digital format.

If you enjoyed this guide, we would love for you to leave us a review wherever you purchased this guide from. Your reviews make a huge difference!

Thank you and have a magical trip!

- G Costa

P.S. Please make sure to use the maps on the following two pages.

Photo credits:
The following photos have been used from Flickr (unless otherwise stated) in this guide under a Creative Commons license. Thank you to: Main front castle image and Big Thunder splash (cover)- Thomas Evraert; Pirate Galleon - Joan Costa; Eurostar (small) - 'kismihok; Eurostar (large) - Philip Sheldrake; Thunder Mesa Riverboat, Blanche Neige and La Cabane des Robinson, Newport bay close, Dumbo, Phantom Manor, Indiana Jones, Peter Pan, it's a small world, Wild West Show - Loren Javier; Dumbo & Pinocchio - Jeremy Thompson; Nautilus - Paul Beattie; Star Tours - Anna Fox; and Ratatouille exterior - Eleazar; Fastpass (single) - Joel; Fastpass (multiple) - JJ Merelo; View of Lake Disney (La Marina section) - Nicola; Val d'Europe - Tves Jalabert; Davy Crockett's Adventure - aventure-aventure.com; Golf - DisneylandParis.com; Aerial Image - Apple Maps; Disney Dollars - R Reeves; Teacups - Kabayanmark Images; Newport Bay far - Nicola; New York Hotel - .Martin.; Crush parade float - Moto@Club4AG; Sleeping Beauty Castle - Sergey Galyonkin; BTM and Halloween - Kevin Marshall; Tower of Terror - Ken Lund; Ratatouille - Martin Lewison; Parachute Drop - Ludovic; Panoramagique - Victor R Ruiz; Eiffel Tower - Pedro Szekely.

Some images are copyright The Walt Disney Company, Disneyland Paris and EuroDisney SCA and used under Fair Use for reporting.

Disneyland Park Map

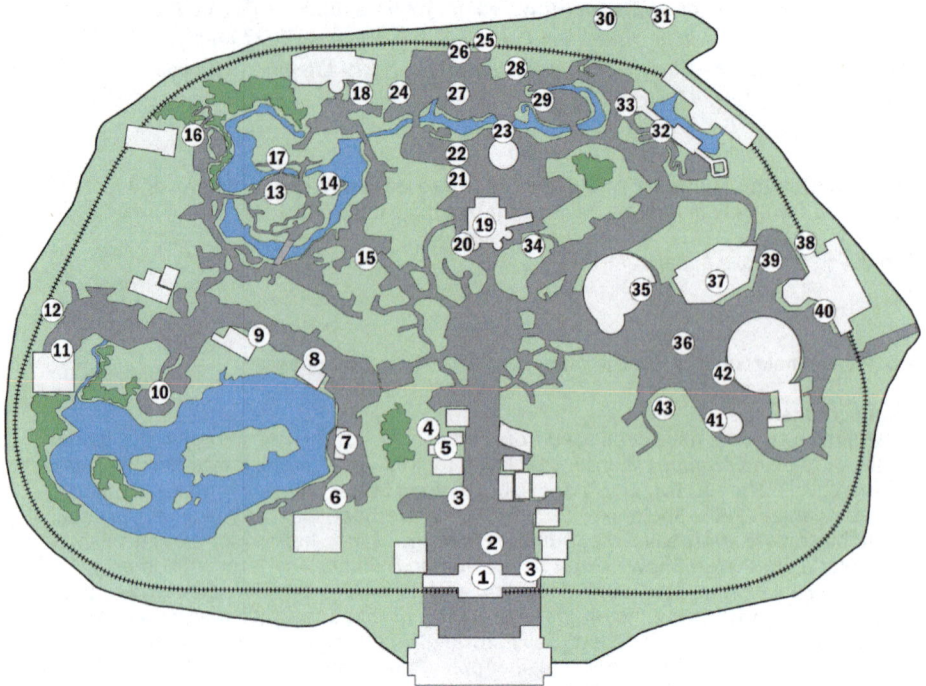

MAIN STREET, U.S.A.
1 - Main Street, U.S.A. Station
2 - Horse-Drawn Streetcars
3 - Main Street Vehicles
4 - Liberty Arcade (Statue of Liberty Tableau)
5 - Dapper Dan's Hair Cuts

FRONTIERLAND
6 - Phantom Manor
7 - Thunder Mesa Riverboat Landing
8 - Rustler Roundup Shooting Gallery (extra charge)
9 - Big Thunder Mountain
10 - Pocahontas Indian Village
11 - Frontierland Theatre (Lion King: Rhythms of the Pride Lands)
12 - Frontierland Station

ADVENTURELAND
13 - La Cabane des Robinson (Treehouse)
14 - Pirates' Beach
15 - Le Passage Enchanté d'Aladdin
16 - Indiana Jones et le Temple du Péril
17 - Adventure Isle
18 - Pirates of the Caribbean

FANTASYLAND
19 - Sleeping Beauty Castle
20 - Dragon's Lair
21 - Snow White and the Seven Dwarfs
22 - Pinocchio's Fantastic Journey
23 - Le Carrousel de Lancelot
24 - Peter Pan's Flight
25 - Fantasyland Station
26 - Meet Mickey
27 - Dumbo: The Flying Elephant
28 - Alice's Curious Labyrinth
29 - Mad Hatter's Tea Cups
30 - Casey Jr. - le Petit Train du Cirque
31 - Storybook Canal Boats/Le Pays des Contes de Fées
32 - "it's a small world"
33 - Princess Pavilion
34 - Castle Stage

DISCOVERYLAND
35 - Buzz Lightyear Laser Blast
36 - Orbitron
37 - Videopolis
38 - Discoveryland Station
39 - Star Tours
40 - Discoveryland Theatre
41 - Les Mystères du Nautilus
42 - Star Wars Hyperspace Mountain
43 - Autopia

Walt Disney Studios Park Map

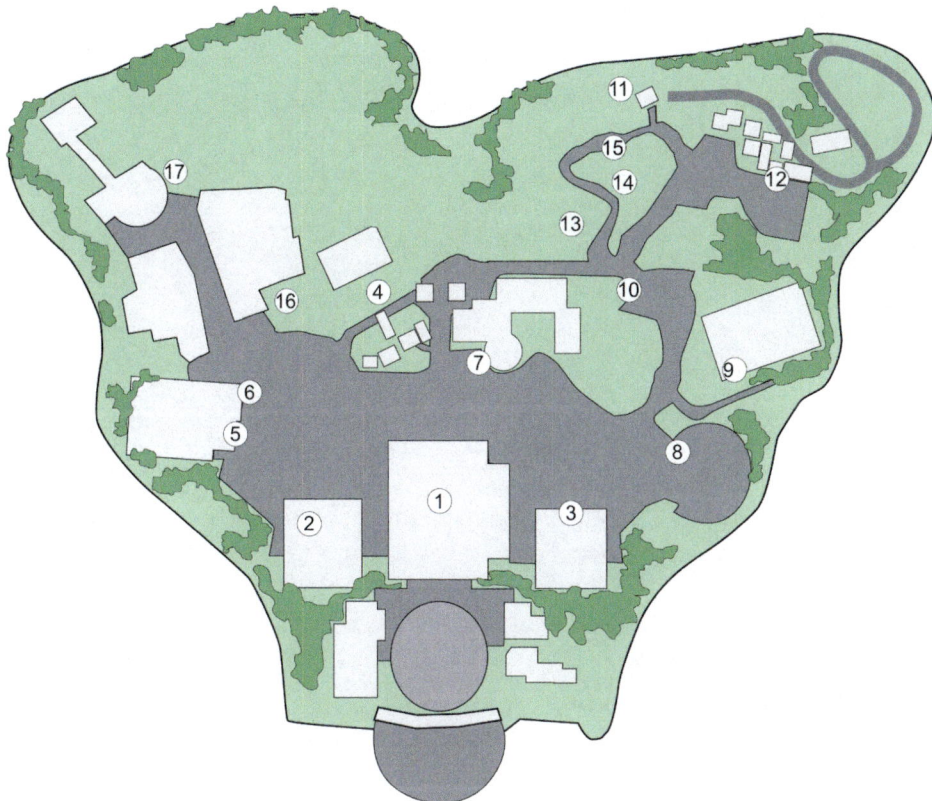

FRONT LOT
1 - Disney Studio 1

PRODUCTION COURTYARD
2 - CineMagique Theatre (showing
Together: a Pixar Musical Adventure)
3 - Animagique Theatre (showing Mickey
and the Magician)
4 - The Twilight Zone: Tower of Terror
5 - Studio D
6 - Stitch Live!

TOON STUDIO AND WORLDS OF PIXAR
7 - Frozen: A Musical Invitation
8 - Flying Carpets over Agrabah

9 - Crush's Coaster
10 - Cars Race Rallye
11 - Cars Road Trip
12 - Ratatouille: The Adventure

TOY STORY PLAYLAND
13 - Toy Soldiers Parachute Drop
14 - Slinky Dog Zig Zag Spin
15 - RC Racer

AVENGERS CAMPUS
16 - Spider-Man W.E.B. Adventure
17 - Avengers Assemble: Flight Force

Printed in Great Britain
by Amazon

58605610R00056